IN & OUT OF THE KITCHEN

in fifteen minutes or less

Anne Willan
IN & OUT OF THE KITCHEN

in fifteen minutes or less

PHOTOGRAPHY BY SARA TAYLOR

QUADRILLE PUBLISHING

half title KEDGEREE *see page 64*
previous pages TAGLIATELLE WITH CORIANDER & GINGER *see page 67*
opposite MOROCCAN DRIED FRUIT & CHOCOLATE GALETTES *see page 112*

To the Cherniavsky kitchen trio, Mark, Simon and Emma

Both metric and imperial quantities are given. Use either all metric or all imperial, as the two are not necessarily interchangeable.

Publishing Director: Anne Furniss
Art Director: Mary Evans
Editor & Project Manager: Lewis Esson
Photography: Sara Taylor
Styling: Penny Markham
Food Styling: Roz Denny, and Jane Suthering assisted by Emma Patmore
Editorial Assistant: Penny David
Design Assistant: Ian Muggeridge

First published in 1995 by
Quadrille Publishing Limited
27–31 Charing Cross Road
London WC2H 0LS

This paperback edition first pubished in 1998

Text © 1995 Anne Willan Inc.
Photography © 1995 Sara Taylor
Design & Layout © 1995 Quadrille Publishing Limited

Cataloguing in Publication Data: a catalogue record for this book is available from the British Library

ISBN 1 899988 67 X

Typesetting by Ian Muggeridge, London
Printed and bound in Singapore

CONTENTS

INTRODUCTION

None of us has much time to spend in the kitchen, yet we all love to eat well. The recipes in this book are my personal solution to the problem, the way I cook myself. With all of them you'll be *In and Out of the Kitchen in Fifteen Minutes or Less*, free to relax while the dish simmers, bakes in the oven or chills in the refrigerator. For some of the recipes, you need not wait at all but can go straight to the table.

You'll see at once that this is real food, made with market-fresh ingredients – dishes such as Chicory Salad with Goats' Cheese Toasts and Roast Pork Loin with Baker's Potatoes, both of them favourites of mine. Now that there's so much fresh produce available all year round, and so many exotic flavourings which were not in our shops a decade ago, we have plenty to play with. It's the way I've been cooking for years, ever since I started balancing a husband, two children and a busy professional life. There's no need to compromise with ready-prepared, packaged goods which are often expensive and always inferior in taste.

However, if you do want to be in and out of the kitchen in a quarter of an hour, you'll need to be organized and keep a Well-stocked Store-cupboard (see page 8). Every second counts – in fact, these recipes were tested stage by stage using a stop-watch. I soon realized we were engaged in critical path analysis, plotting the shortest way of putting the ingredients together from start to finish. To help chart the way, I've had invaluable help from Alex Bird, an experienced La Varenne chef, and from Amanda Hesser, Marah Stets and Kevin Tyldesley, all aspiring cooks. What they can achieve, so can you.

Throughout the book, I've concentrated on dishes which are substantial enough to anchor a menu with little or no accompaniment. There's a choice of traditional and innovative Wholes-in-one, several ideas On the Light Side, some of which are vegetarian, plus Speedy Salads and a group of recipes which take you only 15 minutes to get to the table. The remaining chapters on starters and desserts offer some quick ways to round off a meal. On page 126 I also suggest some menus combining recipes from different chapters in the book.

What won't you find here? No breads and few pastries or cakes, as they require far too much work. Roast meats need basting and are finished with a sauce or gravy, so don't meet our '15 minutes then relax' rule. Nor do we feature elaborate last-minute decorations or plate presentations. However, I think you'll be surprised by the range of possible dishes, from Fifteen-minute Minestrone to Chicken in Chilli Coconut Sauce, or Roast Root Vegetables with Walnuts and a Plum Batter Pudding.

This is my style of cooking and my kind of food. With this book I welcome you into my kitchen, hoping you enjoy it as much as I do. All I'm asking for is 15 minutes of your time!

left PLUM BATTER PUDDING *see page 109*

How to Use This Book

The recipes in this book give you a good deal of background, for instance advice on choosing ingredients and finding substitutes, or what to look out for in a tricky technique. If you've already been successful with a dish, for a repeat performance you should only need to consult the ingredient list and the Recap notes at the end.

Quantities are geared to serve four. If you're a smaller party – two, or even solo – you're not going to save much time by reducing quantities, and you may compromise results as ingredient amounts do not necessarily change in direct proportion to servings. You'll be much better off enjoying a few leftovers the following day. For flexibility, I've indicated dishes which reheat well and those which are easy to make in large quantities.

In saving time, we have to cut some corners. Vegetables are rarely peeled, so you'll find lots of earthy texture and taste. If produce is available in your market already washed, go for it. As I often suggest in my recipe introductions, wherever possible get the fishmonger or butcher to fillet, clean and slice things for you.

Quite a number of recipes call for a food processor or mixer – both great time-savers. I'd opt for a different recipe if you don't have either machine. The microwave I find less useful, but I do suggest it as an alternative in a dozen or so recipes where you can save significant time without spoiling the outcome.

Finally, you'll find two procedures cannot be hurried – heating the oven and boiling a pan of water, so often I ask you to do this before starting the recipe.

The Well-stocked Store-cupboard

Everyone's idea of a well-stocked store-cupboard differs, and here is mine. All the items can be kept for weeks or months so they are true store-cupboard ingredients. I'm not suggesting by any means that you need all of the following ingredients. They are food for thought before we go into the kitchen.

Basics
Even the most modest college dorm or bachelor studio surely stocks:

Salt, black pepper (ready ground or in a mill), *flour, granulated sugar, vegetable oil, tea* and *coffee.*

Add some options with *ground white pepper, black peppercorns, brown* and *caster sugar.*

Flavourings
Here's where the fun begins:

Vinegars can run to *red* and *white wine, cider, rice, raspberry* and *balsamic.*

Oils may include *olive, walnut,* and *dark sesame oil* for an Oriental touch.

For salty and piquant flavour, there's a choice of *soy, Worcestershire* and *Tabasco sauces, capers, anchovies, sun-dried tomatoes, horseradish* and *Dijon mustard,* before we even start to look at Oriental possibilities, such as *oyster, fish* and *plum sauces.*

For desserts, don't forget *vanilla essence* and *pods.*

Spices and herbs
It's amazing how many dried spices and herbs we are now accustomed to using.

Aromatic spices start with *nutmeg, ground* and *stick cinnamon, whole* and *ground allspice* and *coriander, ground* and *seed cumin.*

For colour, look towards *saffron, turmeric* and *paprika.*

For heat you need *dry mustard, ginger* and the *chilli* family – *dried hot red pepper* or *red pepper flakes, cayenne pepper* and *red chilli paste.*

As for dried herbs, I find only a few retain their aroma – small jars of *bay leaf, rosemary, thyme* and *sage* do well.

For other herbs, fresh sprigs have far more flavour and will keep for about a week in the refrigerator. I don't go much for mixes, except for *Provençal herbs* and, of course, *curry powder.*

GRAINS AND PASTA

Our family tastes turn to grains rather than pasta, so we rarely stock more than:

Dried spaghetti, macaroni or *fusilli, tagliatelle* and perhaps some *Oriental rice noodles.*

We're much more adventurous with grains, so you can count on finding *cracked wheat, bulgur, kasha, couscous* and *polenta* among the *rice — long-grain white rice, basmati, wild* and probably *brown rice* as well.

Add a few oddments, such as *lentils* and *rolled oats* and you've the basis of dozens of meals right there.

DRIED FRUITS, NUTS AND PRESERVES

Here's where sweetness and texture come from, starting with:

Raisins, prunes, dried apricots, figs and *dates,* and my favourite *candied orange* and *ginger* for cakes.

My cupboard is always full of nuts — *walnuts, pecans, hazelnuts* (preferably peeled as well as shelled), shelled and blanched *pistachios, pine nuts,* and a slew of *almonds,* whole, blanched, slivered and ground. *Peanut butter,* too.

This is a good place to mention *redcurrant jelly* and *apricot jam,* for glazing fruit tarts, plus a pot of *citrus marmalade* and hopefully some *home-made jam* for the breakfast toast.

Last, and most important of all, are *honey* and *bittersweet chocolate,* the basis of so many contemporary desserts.

CANS

You'll find few cans in our house, just some whole *tomatoes* (preferably *plum*) and *tomato paste,* in a tube so it keeps better after opening. I find *white kidney beans* useful for adding body to vegetable soup, with some cans of *low-salt veal* and *chicken stock* for emergency. That's it.

THE FREEZER

Now here's much more scope for creativity. Let's put aside the freezer as a place to store leftovers, and concentrate on ingredients. In our freezer there's always a back-up supply of *fresh tagliatelle, butter* and *grated Parmesan* or *Gruyère cheese.* We add our own *fresh peas, green beans* and other garden vegetables, but the only commercially frozen produce I ever buy is *leaf spinach* and *raspberries.* Add *sliced white* or *brown bread* (for toast), *filo pastry* (too difficult to make fresh), thinly sliced *bacon* (because we love it), and a tub or two of *ice-cream,* and here are the store-cupboard contents of our freezer. You, I am sure, have lots of your own ideas.

FRESH PRODUCE

Now we enter the realm of the working kitchen — the following items will last a week or two, depending on the temperature of your kitchen. In your standby vegetable rack I would hope to find *potatoes* and roots such as *carrots,* and perhaps *turnip, leeks* or *celery.* The onion family — *Spanish onions, sweet red, spring onions* or *white onions* for salad, and *garlic* — are indispensable. Some shallots would be helpful, as would a chunk of *fresh root ginger.* And you must include some citrus fruit — *oranges, lemons* and *limes.*

THE REFRIGERATOR

We look here for dairy produce, including *butter, milk, cream, eggs, yogurt, sour cream* and *cream cheese.*

THE DRINKS CUPBOARD

Never overlook the possibilities of alcohol in the kitchen. Starting with *red* and *white wine,* we move to fortified wines such as *Marsala, Madeira, sherry* and *Port.* A dash of spirits — *Cognac, rum,* or *whisky* and maybe a lesser-known type such as *Calvados* or *Pernod* — lifts many a ragout and sauce (only vodka has little to offer in the way of background taste). White alcohols such as *kirsch* and *poire* (pear brandy) do well in desserts, as do liqueurs like orange-based *Grand Marnier* or *Cointreau.*

OFF TO A QUICK START

Rarely do we forgo a starter at home, even if it's only a green salad sprinkled with cheese or chopped walnuts. I think of an appetizer as setting the stage for a meal, raising expectations and leading without fuss into the main course. Or, that's the way it should be.

As always, I like to be organized. Each recipe has its place. If we have guests, then the appetizer must be easy to make ahead, so I can focus on the main dishes without interruption. Smoked Salmon or Mackerel Rillettes, or a Chicken Liver & Apple Mousse are ideal for a party. On a warm evening, we may relax by ourselves with a chilled Melon Salad with Balsamic Vinegar, while on winter days Italian Escarole Soup makes a welcome opening. Both take less than 10 minutes' preparation and are ready to eat almost at once. As a Saturday treat, Potted Shrimps are a weakness of ours, consumed in double helpings with a glass of good Chardonnay.

In fact, good appetizers are so attractive that in restaurants I don't hesitate to have two, or even three, forgetting the main course altogether. I wouldn't suggest you do that here, unless you have time to spare. You will find, however, that recipes such as Salmon Carpaccio can form a pleasant summer meal when supplemented by a green salad and a fresh loaf of your favourite bread.

left RED WINE GAZPACHO *see page 12*

RED WINE GAZPACHO

TIME IN KITCHEN
9 minutes
CHILLING *at least
2 hours*
STORAGE *up to 24 hours
in the refrigerator*

serves 4

2 slices of white bread
500 g / 1 lb very ripe
   large tomatoes, or
   more if needed
1 red pepper
½ medium cucumber
1 garlic clove
4 tablespoons olive oil
125 ml / 4 fl oz red
   wine
3 tablespoons red wine
   vinegar, or more if
   needed
pinch of sugar
salt and freshly ground
   black pepper
ice cubes, for serving

food processor

To call gazpacho a liquid salad is banal, but the expression does sum up the appeal of this chilled Spanish soup. Like any salad, prime ingredients — in this case, ripe tomatoes, red pepper and cucumber — show at their best.

With a food processor, it is just possible to use fresh tomatoes and keep within our time limit, but I know canned tomatoes are a time-saving temptation — I leave it to you.

Careful seasoning of the soup with olive oil, red wine vinegar and some fruity red wine is important. Above all, gazpacho *is refreshing in summer heat, so be sure it is thoroughly chilled and add an ice cube to each bowl just before serving.*

Put bread in a small bowl, pour over 250 ml / 8 fl oz of cold water and leave to soak.

Next, prepare the vegetables for puréeing in the food processor. The aim here is to remove as many cores, seeds and skins as possible in a short time — the texture of the soup is still going to be slightly rough. Very healthy!

With the point of a knife, scoop out and discard the cores from the tomatoes. Cut across in half, squeeze out the seeds and cut the flesh into large chunks. Halve the pepper, snap out the cores and discard the seeds. Cut the flesh into quarters. Peel the cucumber with a vegetable peeler, keeping 4 thin strips of peel for garnish. Cut it in half lengthwise and scoop out the seeds with a teaspoon. Cut the cucumber into chunks. With the flat of the knife, lightly crush the garlic clove to loosen the skin and discard.

Add half the vegetables to the food processor and purée them as smoothly as possible. Pour this vegetable purée into a large bowl.

Squeeze the soaked bread in your hands to remove excess water. Purée the rest of the vegetables with the olive oil and bread and add to the bowl.

Stir in the wine, vinegar, sugar and salt and pepper. Taste for seasoning: how much depends very much on the vegetables. Cover and chill the gazpacho for at least 2 hours.

Stir the gazpacho: it should be quite thick, but add a little more water if it seems too heavy. Taste it again, adding more seasoning and possibly more vinegar to pick up the fresh flavour. Spoon into serving bowls, add an ice cube and top each bowl with one of the strips of cucumber peel, tied in a knot.

RECAP

1 PUT BREAD IN A SMALL BOWL, POUR OVER 250 ML / 8 FL OZ WATER AND LEAVE TO SOAK.

2 CORE TOMATOES, HALVE AND SCOOP OUT SEEDS. CUT INTO LARGE CHUNKS. HALVE PEPPER, REMOVE CORE AND SEEDS AND CUT INTO QUARTERS. PEEL CUCUMBER, KEEPING 4 THIN STRIPS FOR GARNISH. HALVE CUCUMBER LENGTHWISE AND SCOOP OUT SEEDS. CUT FLESH INTO CHUNKS. PEEL GARLIC.

3 SQUEEZE SOAKED BREAD TO REMOVE EXCESS WATER. PURÉE VEGETABLES IN FOOD PROCESSOR IN TWO BATCHES, ADDING OLIVE OIL AND BREAD TO LAST BATCH.

4 STIR IN WINE, VINEGAR, SUGAR, SALT AND PEPPER. TASTE FOR SEASONING.

5 COVER AND CHILL AT LEAST 2 HOURS.

6 IF NECESSARY, THIN SOUP WITH LITTLE MORE WATER AND ADJUST SEASONING. SPOON INTO BOWLS, ADD ICE CUBE AND TOP WITH KNOTTED STRIP OF CUCUMBER PEEL.

ITALIAN ESCAROLE SOUP

TIME IN KITCHEN
  7 minutes
SIMMERING *10-15 minutes*
  (5-6 in the microwave)
STORAGE *up to 24 hours*
  in the refrigerator
serves 4

small head of escarole
  (about 500 g / 1 lb)
1 litre / 1⅔ pt chicken
  or vegetable stock
2 garlic cloves
2 tablespoons olive oil
small bunch of basil
250 g / 8 oz can of
  cooked white kidney
  beans
salt and freshly ground
  black pepper

Italians love to sauté escarole with garlic and olive oil, for serving as a hot vegetable. With the addition of chicken stock and some white beans, you have a savoury soup, delicious served with cheese straws or a sprinkling of grated Parmesan cheese.

If escarole — also sold as Batavian endive — is not available, you can substitute curly chicory, which has slightly thicker leaves than frisée. For a richer version of this dish, add a lightly beaten egg to the boiling soup just before serving, stirring rapidly so that the egg cooks to thin ribbons in the liquid.

Bring the stock to the boil in a covered pan.

With the flat of a knife, lightly crush the garlic cloves to loosen and remove the skin. Smash the cloves with the flat of the knife, then chop them with the blade.

Heat the oil in a soup pan, add the garlic and cook gently for 1-2 minutes until soft. Take care it does not scorch or it will be bitter.

Meanwhile, discard the tough green outer leaves from the escarole, trim the stem and pull the inner leaves apart. If they are dirty, wash them in a sink full of cold water. There is no need to dry them. Chop them with a large knife, cutting more or less coarsely, depending how much texture you like in your soup. The leaves will, of course, wilt and lose much of their bulk during cooking.

Add the chopped escarole to the soup pan with some salt and pepper. Sauté for 1-2 minutes.

Meanwhile, strip the basil leaves from the stems. Stack the leaves, roll them loosely and cut them into strips, taking care not to bruise them by chopping too finely.

Add the boiling stock to the soup pan, cover and simmer for 10-15 minutes, until the escarole is tender.

Stir in the beans with their liquid and bring the soup just back to the boil.

For an even shorter cooking time using the microwave, pour the soup into a microwave bowl. Cover with microwave film and cook on high for 5 minutes. Add the beans and microwave for 45 seconds longer.

When the soup is cooked, stir in the basil, taste it for seasoning and serve.

RECAP

1 BRING STOCK TO BOIL IN COVERED PAN.

2 PEEL AND CHOP GARLIC. HEAT OIL IN SOUP PAN AND COOK GARLIC GENTLY UNTIL SOFT.

3 MEANWHILE, DISCARD TOUGH OUTER GREEN LEAVES FROM ESCAROLE, TRIM STEM AND PULL INNER LEAVES APART. IF DIRTY, WASH. DEPENDING ON TEXTURE YOU WANT, CHOP LEAVES COARSELY OR MORE FINELY.

4 ADD ESCAROLE TO SOUP PAN WITH SALT AND PEPPER. SAUTÉ 1-2 MINUTES.

5 MEANWHILE, STRIP BASIL LEAVES FROM STEMS AND COARSELY CHOP.

6 ADD BOILING STOCK TO SOUP PAN, COVER AND SIMMER 10-15 MINUTES, UNTIL ESCAROLE IS TENDER.

7 STIR IN BEANS WITH THEIR LIQUID AND BRING JUST BACK TO BOIL.

* ALTERNATIVELY, COOK IN MICROWAVE IN A COVERED BOWL, ALLOWING 5 MINUTES AT HIGH. STIR IN BEANS AND COOK 45 SECONDS LONGER.

8 STIR IN BASIL, ADJUST SEASONING AND SERVE.

ANGELS & DEVILS ON HORSEBACK

TIME IN KITCHEN
10 minutes
GRILLING *8 minutes*

serves 4

8 **thin slices of bacon**
(about 250 g / ½ lb)
8 **shelled medium**
oysters
(about 100 g / 3¼ oz)
8 **pitted ready-to-eat**
prunes
(about 60 g / 2 oz)
4 **slices of white bread**
30 g / 1 oz **unsalted**
butter
½ **teaspoon**
Worcestershire
sauce, or more to
taste

8 wooden cocktail sticks

Angels and devils on horseback are an evocative description for bacon rolls filled with oysters and prunes, set on a 'horse' of toast. Scallops can make alternative angels, or chicken livers may replace prunes as devils. Together they make a classic Victorian savoury, served at the end of a hearty dinner after dessert, and designed to tickle the palate and tease the imagination. You'll only find savouries now in London clubs and at university high tables, where they are slotted in before the appearance of port and brandy. As an addict of crispy bacon, I've always loved angels and devils on horseback, not as a savoury I must confess, but as a cocktail hors d'oeuvre or a first course.

Preheat the grill and cover the grill rack with foil – allow 5 minutes for this before you begin the recipe.

Cut the bacon slices in half. Roll a piece of bacon around each oyster and each prune. You'll find the oysters are tiresomely slippery, but prunes are more amenable. Spear an oyster and a prune on each of 8 wooden cocktail sticks, setting them on the foil.

Grill the rolls about 5 cm / 2 in away from the heat – quite close – so the bacon browns, but the oysters do not overcook and remain soft.

After about 2 minutes, turn the skewers and continue grilling for 2-3 minutes more, until the bacon is brown. If you are using fatty bacon, it should be crisp and the fat should be rendered.

Meanwhile, toast the bread in a toaster. Melt the butter and add the Worcestershire sauce. Once the bread is toasted, cut off the crusts and cut each slice in half.

Brush the flavoured butter on the bread and set 2 pieces of bread on each of 4 warmed plates. Top with the angels and devils and serve very hot.

RECAP

1 PREHEAT GRILL AND COVER GRILL RACK WITH FOIL – ALLOW **5** MINUTES FOR THIS BEFORE YOU START.

2 HALVE BACON SLICES AND ROLL AROUND OYSTERS AND PRUNES. SPEAR AN OYSTER AND A PRUNE ON EACH OF **8** WOODEN COCKTAIL STICKS AND SET ON FOIL.

3 GRILL ABOUT **2** MINUTES CLOSE TO HEAT SO BACON BROWNS FAST AND OYSTERS DO NOT OVERCOOK. TURN AND GRILL OTHER SIDE FOR **2-3** MINUTES UNTIL BACON IS CRISP.

4 MEANWHILE, TOAST BREAD. MELT BUTTER AND ADD WORCESTERSHIRE SAUCE. TRIM CRUSTS OF TOASTS AND HALVE EACH SLICE. BRUSH WITH BUTTER AND SET ON **4** WARMED PLATES.

5 TOP WITH SKEWERS OF ANGELS AND DEVILS AND SERVE VERY HOT.

CHICKEN LIVER
& APPLE MOUSSE

TIME IN KITCHEN
  10 minutes
CHILLING *at least 4 hours*
STORAGE *up to 3 days*
  in the refrigerator if
  sealed with butter
serves *4-6*

**125 g / 4 oz chicken
  livers**
**60 g / 2 oz unsalted
  butter**
1 dessert apple
2 shallots
**2 tablespoons Calvados
  or Cognac**
**salt and freshly ground
  black pepper**

food processor
earthenware pot or
  4 individual ramekins

Cheap and plentiful chicken livers — who would have thought so much good could come from a battery chicken? Why not sauté chicken livers to top a green salad, wrap them in bacon as an alternative to prunes in Angels & Devils on Horseback (see page 14), or add a bit of apple to make this simple mousse? The key is flaming with Calvados (apple brandy) or with Cognac to cut the richness of the livers. The mousse is easy to make in larger quantities and it keeps well, up to 3 days if you seal it with a thin layer of melted butter. French bread is the appropriate accompaniment for a recipe of such Gallic pedigree.

Cut the chicken livers into 2 or 3 pieces, discarding any membrane. If they are wet (a sign they have been frozen and will have less taste), dry them well on paper towels.

Melt half the butter in a frying pan, add the livers and sprinkle them with salt and pepper. Leave them to sauté over medium heat.

Meanwhile, peel the apple, cut it in quarters and cut out the core. Thinly slice the quarters into the pan of livers and stir to mix them. Leave them to continue cooking, turning up the heat if the livers have not started to brown nicely.

With a small knife, peel the shallots, leaving a little of the root. Cut them in half from stem to root and set them cut side down on the chopping board. Thinly slice them and add to the chicken livers.

Stir, turn the heat to high and cook for about 2 minutes longer until the livers are well browned, though they should still be pink in the centre. Never mind if the shallot is still a bit crisp.

Take the pan from the heat, pour over the Calvados or Cognac and light it with a match, standing back so your eyebrows are not singed. If it does not light, put it back over the heat and try again.

Tip the contents of the pan into the food processor and add the remaining butter. Purée until smooth. Season the mousse to taste, adding a generous amount of pepper. Spoon it into an earthenware pot or individual dishes.

Smooth the top with a knife, cover and chill it for at least 4 hours. I like to serve the mousse chilled.

RECAP

1 CUT CHICKEN LIVERS INTO 2-3 PIECES, DISCARDING ANY MEMBRANE. DRY WELL.

2 MELT HALF BUTTER IN FRYING PAN AND ADD LIVERS WITH SALT AND PEPPER. LEAVE TO SAUTÉ OVER MEDIUM HEAT.

3 PEEL, QUARTER, CORE AND SLICE APPLE INTO PAN WITH LIVERS.

4 PEEL AND THINLY SLICE SHALLOTS AND ADD TO PAN. TURN UP HEAT AND CONTINUE COOKING ABOUT 2 MINUTES UNTIL LIVERS ARE BROWN BUT STILL PINK IN CENTRE.

5 TAKE PAN FROM HEAT, ADD CALVADOS OR COGNAC AND FLAME.

6 TIP CONTENTS OF PAN INTO FOOD PROCESSOR, ADD REMAINING BUTTER AND PURÉE UNTIL SMOOTH. SEASON MOUSSE TO TASTE, ADDING PLENTY OF PEPPER, AND SPOON IT INTO AN EARTHENWARE POT OR INDIVIDUAL DISHES.

7 SMOOTH TOP WITH A KNIFE, COVER AND CHILL AT LEAST 4 HOURS.

POTTED SHRIMPS

TIME IN KITCHEN
7-8 minutes
CHILLING at least
2 hours
STORAGE up to 2 days in
the refrigerator

serves 4

500 g / 1 lb peeled cooked shrimps or prawns
½ teaspoon freshly grated nutmeg
cayenne pepper
75 g / 2½ oz unsalted butter
salt and freshly ground black pepper
1 lemon, to serve

wok and stirrer
earthenware pot or
4 individual ramekins

This recipe is one of my all-time favourites. Potting is akin to what the French do when making confit, *an ancient way of preserving food by spicing and baking it very thoroughly to destroy bacteria, then sealing it with a generous layer of fat (preferably butter in this case). Shellfish does particularly well, the spice and butter accenting its sweet flavour. Many a pot of shrimps and glass of dry sherry have I shared with my father beside the winter fire.*

The following recipe will be instantly personalized by the type of shrimp or prawn you use. Ordinary prawns are fine — please look for some that are freshly cooked, not frozen. Pink baby shrimps are even better, and best of all the tasty grey or bay shrimps.

For speed, I like to use a wok. For more flavour, I toast the butter to the 'hazelnut' stage, so that the milk solids evaporate and brown, adding a delicious nutty taste.

If you are using prawns, coarsely chop them in the food processor. Baby shrimps should be left whole. Put the prawns or shrimps in a bowl and sprinkle with the nutmeg, a '*pointe*' of cayenne (measured by dipping in the point of a small knife), salt and a generous amount of black pepper. Stir well.

Melt the butter in the wok and place over a medium heat for 20-30 seconds, until the bubbling stops and it starts to colour slightly; you'll see little golden specks in it.

Meanwhile, trim the ends from the lemon and cut it into 8 wedges.

As soon as the butter is ready, turn up the heat, add the prawns or shrimps and stir-fry briskly with the wok stirrer, spreading them over the whole surface of the pan. Cook over a very high heat for 1-2 minutes, until they start to brown.

If they do not brown but start to leak liquid, it is a sign either that they had been frozen or that the heat was too low. Tip them into a strainer and discard the liquid. Reheat the wok until very hot, add the prawns or shrimps and cook until brown.

Take the pan from the heat and season the prawns or shrimps to taste with salt, pepper and more nutmeg — they should be quite spicy, and they will seem blander when they are cold. Pile them in an earthenware pot or individual ramekins and leave at least 2 hours in the refrigerator so that the butter sets. If you are in a hurry or it's a cold night, however, the shrimps are also delicious hot.

Whether hot or cold, serve them with wedges of lemon, accompanied by a crusty whole-wheat loaf or toasted whole-wheat bread.

RECAP

1 IF USING PRAWNS, COARSELY CHOP IN THE FOOD PROCESSOR. LEAVE LITTLE SHRIMPS WHOLE. MIX PRAWNS OR SHRIMPS IN A BOWL WITH NUTMEG, A 'POINTE' OF CAYENNE, SALT AND PLENTY OF PEPPER.

2 HEAT BUTTER IN WOK AND COOK 20-30 SECONDS UNTIL HAZELNUT-BROWN.

3 MEANWHILE, TRIM ENDS FROM LEMON AND CUT INTO 8 WEDGES.

4 WHEN BUTTER IS READY, ADD PRAWNS OR SHRIMPS AND STIR-FRY BRISKLY 1-2 MINUTES UNTIL THEY START TO BROWN.

5 TAKE FROM THE HEAT AND SEASON TO TASTE — THEY SHOULD BE QUITE

SPICY. PILE IN A POT OR INDIVIDUAL RAMEKINS.

6 THE SHRIMPS CAN BE SERVED HOT, OR CHILL FOR AT LEAST 2 HOURS. SERVE WITH WEDGES OF LEMON, ACCOMPANIED BY WHOLE-WHEAT BREAD OR TOAST.

SALMON CARPACCIO

TIME IN KITCHEN
10 minutes
MARINATING *15-30*
minutes in the
refrigerator

serves 4 as an appetizer,
or 2 as a main course

500 g / 1 lb fillet of
salmon with the skin
2 lemons
4 tablespoons olive oil
small bunch of chives
2 tablespoons capers
3-4 sprigs of flat-leaf
parsley
salt and freshly ground
black pepper

Originally denoting marinated raw beef, the Italian term 'carpaccio' now has been stretched to cover rich fish in the raw, such as salmon and tuna, with all sorts of toppings. Whatever the main ingredient, I believe the flavourings should hark back to Italy — olive oil, capers, chopped flat-leaf parsley and perhaps some chives. Most important is the lemon juice, the acidity of which whitens and slightly 'cooks' the raw fish. Just a few minutes' marinating is enough to heighten the flavour of salmon.

Of course, the fish should be sparkling fresh and sweet-smelling. At a good fish counter, the 'pin' bones running down the centre of the fillet will always be removed — it's a tiresome job to do yourself.

Have ready 4 large serving plates.

Run your fingers over the cut side of the salmon from head to tail; if you feel a line of bones in the centre of the fish, you will need to pull them out with tweezers or using your thumb and a small knife.

To slice the salmon: working away from you towards the tail of the fillet with a very sharp knife, cut the thinnest possible diagonal slices, leaving skin behind. Use a sawing motion with the knife almost parallel to the board — you may not achieve wafer-thin slices first time, but the salmon will still taste good. As you cut the slices, lay them on the plates, covering all but the edges.

Halve the lemons and squeeze the juice of one half lemon over each plate. Drizzle the plates as evenly as possible with olive oil. Then, using a pastry brush, spread the lemon juice and oil to coat the salmon.

Snip the chives with scissors, letting them fall on the fish. Rinse the capers in a small sieve and shake to dry. Sprinkle them over the fish. Strip the parsley leaves from the stems, chop them and sprinkle over the fish. Finally sprinkle the salmon lightly with salt and quite generously with freshly ground pepper. The balance of seasonings for carpaccio is really very much up to you. Some cooks like a fruity oil, others more lemon juice and lots of pepper; it's a very personal dish.

Cover the plates with cling film and chill for 15-30 minutes to marinate. Don't leave the fish much longer as it will lose its fresh flavour.

RECAP

1 REMOVE ANY BONES FROM FILLET AND CUT IN THINNEST POSSIBLE DIAGONAL SLICES, LEAVING SKIN BEHIND. LAY SLICES ON 4 LARGE SERVING PLATES AS YOU GO.

2 HALVE LEMONS AND SPRINKLE EACH PLATE OF SALMON WITH JUICE. DRIZZLE WITH OLIVE OIL

AND BRUSH TO COAT SALMON EVENLY.

3 SNIP CHIVES WITH SCISSORS, LETTING THEM FALL ON FISH. RINSE AND SHAKE DRY CAPERS AND SCATTER OVER FISH. CHOP PARSLEY LEAVES AND SPRINKLE OVER. FINALLY ADD SALT AND PEPPER.

4 COVER WITH CLING FILM AND CHILL 15-30 MINUTES.

SMOKED SALMON RILLETTES

TIME IN KITCHEN
9 minutes
CHILLING at least
2 hours
STORAGE up to 2 days in
the refrigerator

serves 4

125 g / 4 oz boneless
skinless salmon fillet
125 g / 4 oz smoked
salmon, sliced or in
pieces
125 g / 4 oz unsalted
butter
1 lemon
cayenne pepper
¼ teaspoon freshly
grated nutmeg
freshly ground black
pepper

food mixer with 'K' hook
4 ramekins

Traditionally, rillettes are a type of French pâté with a characteristic rough texture. They call for a rich meat like duck or pork, cooked until it flakes and falls from the bone, then puréed. Serve me rillettes, any rillettes, and I'll have a feast. Luckily for my cholesterol levels, cooks have recently started making lighter versions with fish, usually salted or smoked.

Smoked salmon rillettes need not be so very expensive. A little goes a long way, so it's a good recipe to double or triple for a party. If your fish man slices his own smoked salmon, he may have cheaper trimmings. I suggest combining smoked with fresh salmon — this costs less and makes the rillettes milder and lighter.

Rillettes are rich, so an accompaniment of toast or bread is essential. I incline towards melba toast or thinly sliced dark whole-wheat bread.

Put 15 g / ½ oz of the butter with 3 tablespoons of water in a frying pan over medium heat. With a sharp knife, split the salmon fillet horizontally into two thinner fillets, so they will cook more quickly. Spread the salmon and the smoked salmon in the pan with the butter and water. Cover and cook gently for 3-4 minutes, until both types of salmon flake easily. Alternatively, you can save a few minutes by cooking the fish in the microwave.

Cream the remaining butter in a mixer fitted with the 'K' hook. If the butter is straight from the refrigerator, you may want to soften it first in the microwave.

Meanwhile, slice 4 rounds from the lemon and reserve the other half for juice.

Drain the salmon and add it to the butter — don't worry if the heat of the salmon melts the butter, it will set later when the rillettes are chilled. With the mixer on low speed, add what is called in France a 'pointe' of cayenne pepper to the rillettes (to measure a 'pointe', simply dip the tip of a small knife into the cayenne) together with the nutmeg and black pepper. Squeeze in the juice from the half lemon. Be careful to work the salmon for only 2-3 minutes, so it forms the rough purée characteristic of rillettes.

Taste and adjust the seasoning, if necessary. As the salmon is salty, you are unlikely to need more salt. Transfer to a bowl, cover and leave to chill for at least 2 hours, so the butter cools and sets slightly. If left longer, the rillettes will solidify; so if you are storing them overnight, allow to come to room temperature, then stir before serving.

Fill the rillettes into ramekins or small serving dishes, roughing the surface with a fork. Top with a slice of lemon and serve toast or bread separately.

RECAP

1 PUT 15 G / ½ OZ OF BUTTER WITH 3 TABLESPOONS OF WATER IN FRYING PAN OVER MEDIUM HEAT. CUT SALMON FILLET HORIZONTALLY IN TWO. SPREAD SALMON AND SMOKED SALMON IN PAN. COVER AND COOK GENTLY 3-4 MINUTES UNTIL BOTH FLAKE EASILY.

2 CREAM BUTTER IN MIXER USING 'K' HOOK. MEANWHILE, CUT 4 SLICES FROM LEMON AND RESERVE REMAINING HALF.

3 DRAIN COOKED SALMON AND ADD TO BUTTER. WITH MIXER ON, ADD CAYENNE, NUTMEG AND BLACK PEPPER. ADD JUICE FROM HALF LEMON.

4 CONTINUE WORKING SALMON 2-3 MINUTES TO GIVE ROUGH PURÉE. ADJUST SEASONING, COVER AND CHILL AT LEAST 2 HOURS.

5 SERVE IN RAMEKINS OR SERVING DISHES, TOPPED WITH LEMON SLICE AND ACCOMPANIED BY TOAST OR BREAD.

Smoked mackerel can be fatty on its own, but it makes excellent rillettes when seasoned with plenty of lemon juice. In the recipe above, substitute 375 g / 12 oz smoked mackerel fillets for the smoked and fresh salmon; if they are the peppered type, so much the better. The mackerel is already cooked, but to soften it cook it skin side up in butter and water for 2 minutes as described in the salmon recipe. Drain, then flake the mackerel flesh, discarding the skin and carefully removing any bones. Continue as described, flavouring the rillettes generously with nutmeg and lemon juice.

MELON SALAD WITH BALSAMIC VINEGAR

TIME IN KITCHEN
  6 minutes
CHILLING 20 minutes to
  2 hours

serves 4

A fine ripe melon is best left well alone, and this idea for melon salad using seasonal raspberries is so simple I hesitate to call it a recipe. You'll find the hint of balsamic vinegar highlights the sweetness of the fruit — the better the vinegar, the more rounded the fruit flavours will be. There's so little work involved that you can easily make the recipe for as many people as you wish.

Selecting a ripe melon has been made harder by refrigerated transportation, which suppresses the most reliable indicator — the smell. The fragrance of a freshly picked melon at its peak will reach you a yard away; so will any tinge of overripe fermentation or bitter acidity. Lacking any tell-tale aroma, look at the stem of the melon, which should be firm and not too withered. The flower end should show a big — rather than small — round scar, denoting a female melon which is the juicier of the species. Don't forget to press the melon around the scar; it should give slightly but not too much. Pressing may bruise the melon, so don't be caught doing that at the fruit counter!

2 small ripe melons
  (about 500 g / 1 lb
  each)
5 tablespoons balsamic
  vinegar
4 teaspoons sugar, or
  more to taste
250 g / ½ lb raspberries

Mix the vinegar and sugar together in a medium bowl.

Pick over raspberries and wash them only if they are dusty. Add them to the vinegar, toss gently and leave to macerate a few minutes. You'll find the vinegar draws out the raspberry juices even during this short time.

Trim a thin slice from both the stem and flower ends of each melon, so the halves will sit flat, then cut the melons across through their 'equators'. Scoop out the seeds with a spoon and discard them.

Pile the raspberries and juice in the melon halves, cover loosely with film and chill for at least 20 minutes or up to 2 hours.

R E C A P

1 MIX VINEGAR AND SUGAR IN BOWL. PICK OVER RASPBERRIES AND ADD TO BOWL, STIRRING TO MIX.

2 TRIM ENDS OF MELON SO THEY WILL SIT FLAT, CUT THEM IN HALF AND SCOOP OUT SEEDS.

3 FILL WITH RASPBERRIES AND JUICE, COVER LOOSELY WITH FILM AND CHILL AT LEAST 20 MINUTES.

WHOLES-IN-ONE

When I'm planning a menu, here's where I begin. 'Wholes-in-one' recipes are designed to be a full meal, needing – at most – a simple accompaniment of pasta, rice, boiled potatoes, bread or a green salad. Half a dozen dishes in this section, such as Tajine of Chicken with Aubergine and Breton Chaudrée are full meals in themselves. Quite a challenge for only 15 minutes' work!

To me, fish is often a first choice as it cooks quickly and benefits from simple treatment, so that quality and flavour can stand alone. I include half a dozen ideas here to suit different types of fish, and you'll find others in the Fifteen Minutes to Table chapter. It's less the actual fish than its type that is important: rich-fleshed, like salmon; fine-textured, such as sole; or firm, such as tuna. It's much better to forget the name and snap up whatever is sparkling fresh.

Turning to the chicken recipes you can choose between chicken breasts, quick-cooking wings, and even a whole Chicken in a Salt Crust – enormous fun, though it takes a while to cook. Aside from a plain steak, meat in 15 minutes is more of a challenge, but Baked Ham with Apples and Cream does not take long to put together for the oven, nor does Roast Pork Loin with Baker's Potatoes.

This chapter is just a start for main-course ideas. If you're in a hurry, turn to Fifteen Minutes to Table for dishes that are ready at once, such as Spiced Indonesian Stir-fry. You will also find there some substantial vegetarian pasta recipes. If you're looking for something lighter, turn to Speedy Salads and On the Light Side for favourites of mine, such as Chicory Salad with Goats' Cheese Toasts or Plum Tomato & Oregano Frittata. 'À l'attaque!'

left CHICKEN WINGS WITH TOMATOES IN CREAM see page 24

See front jacket

CHICKEN WINGS WITH TOMATOES IN CREAM

TIME IN KITCHEN
   11 minutes
BAKING 15-20 minutes
serves 4

12-16 chicken wings
   (about 1.4 kg / 3 lb)
250 ml / 8 fl oz plain
   yogurt
1 teaspoon salt
½ teaspoon pepper

for the baked tomatoes:
2 large beefsteak
   tomatoes
1 tablespoon olive oil
1 onion
125 ml / 4 fl oz double
   cream
salt and pepper

Given our 15-minute limit on work time, we cannot leave chicken wings to marinate, but you'll find the Middle-Eastern trick of a quick coating of yogurt works wonders. Not only does yogurt add flavour, but it bakes to an agreeable golden brown. Beefsteak tomatoes, browned and finished with cream, make a delicious accompaniment.

Preheat the oven to 260°C/500°F/gas10 or its highest setting if it cannot reach that — allow 5-10 minutes for this before you start the recipe. Line a baking sheet with foil.

Put the yogurt, salt and pepper in a large bowl. Add the chicken wings and, using your hands, mix until they are well coated. Arrange on the baking sheet with the cut joints upwards and spoon over any remaining marinade.

Bake them in the preheated oven, while preparing the tomatoes.

In a small frying pan, gently heat the oil. Peel the onion, leaving a little of the root to hold it together. Cut it in half from stem to root and set it cut side down on a cutting board. Thinly slice it, again cutting from stem to root. Add it to the oil with salt and pepper, stir and leave to cook.

Scoop the cores from the tomatoes with a small knife and cut them across in half. Sprinkle the cut surfaces with salt and pepper.

Heat the onions until very hot. Push them to one side of the pan and add the tomatoes cut side down — they should sizzle and smoke indicating that they have started to cook at once and will brown quickly. If the heat is too low, they may turn mushy. Leave them to cook over a medium heat for 2-3 minutes.

Turn the chicken wings and continue baking them for 15-20 minutes, until brown and very tender. When you try flexing a wing joint, it should move easily.

Turn the tomatoes and continue cooking for 2 minutes more. Add the cream, stirring it into the onions at the side of the pan and spreading them over the bottom. Boil the mixture well and you will find it will thicken slightly to form a lightly caramelized sauce. Cover the pan and set the tomatoes aside to keep warm.

When the chicken wings are done, reheat the tomatoes on top of the stove. Transfer the wings and tomatoes with their sauce to a platter or individual plates.

RECAP

1 PREHEAT OVEN TO 260°C/500°F/GAS10 OR ITS HIGHEST SETTING — ALLOWING 5-10 MINUTES FOR THIS BEFORE YOU START. LINE BAKING SHEET WITH FOIL.

2 PUT YOGURT, SALT AND PEPPER IN A BOWL, ADD CHICKEN AND MIX WELL.

3 ARRANGE ON BAKING SHEET, CUT JOINTS UP. BAKE WHILE PREPARING TOMATOES.

4 GENTLY HEAT OIL IN SMALL FRYING PAN. PEEL AND SLICE ONION, ADD TO OIL WITH SALT AND PEPPER AND LEAVE TO SAUTÉ.

5 CORE AND HALVE TOMATOES. SEASON CUT SIDE. INCREASE HEAT UNDER FRYING PAN AND ADD TOMATOES CUT SIDE DOWN. COOK OVER MODERATE HEAT 2-3 MINUTES.

6 TURN TOMATOES AND CONTINUE COOKING 2 MINUTES. ADD CREAM, STIR INTO ONIONS AND BOIL SO IT THICKENS SLIGHTLY. COVER AND SET ASIDE.

7 TURN CHICKEN WINGS AND CONTINUE BAKING 15-20 MINUTES, UNTIL BROWN AND VERY TENDER.

8 TRANSFER WINGS WITH TOMATOES AND SAUCE TO A PLATTER OR INDIVIDUAL PLATES.

CHICKEN IN A SALT CRUST

TIME IN KITCHEN
5 minutes
BAKING *1¼-1½ hours*
STORAGE *up to 3 days in the refrigerator*

serves 3-4

This is the only recipe I know that calls for just two ingredients — chicken and coarse salt. The chicken is completely covered in salt, almost as if it were coated in snow, and baked. You'll be amazed by its juiciness and lively flavour, much like my favourite duck confit.

I prefer to use kosher salt rather than sea salt, as it is milder and also less expensive than speciality salts like Maldon or Guérlande, which are intended as a table condiment. The baked chicken can be kept refrigerated for several days, but bear in mind that the salt flavour will intensify. If too salty, use the chicken like ham for flavouring other ingredients — an omelette perhaps, or some braised vegetables.

For this recipe, the size of the pot is important — it should be large enough for the chicken not to touch the sides, but if it is any bigger you will need more salt. While the chicken bakes you've plenty of time to make a vegetable accompaniment, such as the Provençal Tricolor of aubergine, tomato and courgette (see page 103), or simply boiled potatoes with melted parsley butter.

1 oven-ready chicken (about 1.8 kg / 4 lb)
2.75 kg / 6 lb kosher or sea salt

deep heatproof casserole
meat thermometer

Preheat the oven to 260°C/500°F/gas10 or its highest possible setting if it cannot reach that — allow 5-10 minutes for this before you start the recipe.

Tie a couple of strings around the chicken so it holds a compact shape and cooks evenly. This also helps prevent too much salt leaking into the cavity.

Spread a 2 cm / ¾ in layer of salt in a deep heatproof casserole. Set the chicken on top and pour over the remaining salt, adding more if necessary so the bird is completely covered by a layer at least 2 cm / ¾ in thick. Be sure to add salt to the chicken only just before baking or juices will be drawn out and the bird will stew rather than browning. If you use a chicken that has been frozen, it may produce a lot of liquid while cooking but this does not matter.

Cover with the lid and bake the chicken in the preheated oven for 1¼ -1½ hours. Insert a meat thermometer through the salt crust into the thickest part of the thigh of the chicken. It should read at least 75°C/170°F. If not, continue cooking for 10-15 minutes more and then test again.

Lift the chicken out of the casserole, shaking it to remove the salt. Using paper towel, rub off any crystals that stick. Set the bird on a platter and carve it at the table.

RECAP

1 PREHEAT OVEN TO 260°C/500°F/GAS10 OR ITS HIGHEST POSSIBLE SETTING IF IT CANNOT REACH THAT — ALLOW 5-10 MINUTES FOR THIS BEFORE YOU START.

2 TIE CHICKEN IN COMPACT SHAPE.

3 SPREAD 2 CM / ¾ IN LAYER OF SALT IN DEEP HEATPROOF CASSEROLE. SET CHICKEN ON TOP AND POUR OVER REMAINING SALT TO FORM 2 CM / ¾ IN LAYER. COVER WITH LID.

4 BAKE 1¼-1½ HOURS. INSERT MEAT THERMOMETER THROUGH CRUST INTO THICKEST PART OF THIGH. IT SHOULD READ AT LEAST 75°C/170°F. IF NOT, CONTINUE COOKING 10-15 MINUTES AND TEST AGAIN.

5 TRANSFER CHICKEN TO PLATTER, DISCARDING SALT, AND CARVE AT TABLE.

CHICKEN IN CHILLI COCONUT SAUCE

TIME IN KITCHEN
  9 minutes
BAKING *40-50 minutes*
STORAGE *2 days in the refrigerator*

serves 4

1 oven-ready chicken, about 1.8 kg / 4 lb, cut into 8 pieces

3 shallots

2 garlic cloves

2 stalks of fresh lemon grass

8 macadamia nuts or 16 blanched almonds

2 teaspoons turmeric

2 teaspoons ground coriander

1 teaspoon ground dried hot red chilli pepper, or to taste

5 tablespoons groundnut or vegetable oil

500 ml / 16 fl oz canned coconut milk

salt

food processor

You can use any part of the chicken in this Indonesian recipe: breasts, thighs, wings or the whole chicken cut into 8 pieces as I suggest here. The sauce gives the chicken a delicious tang — it is quite hot, so cut down on the chilli if you like. Lemon grass is becoming more readily available, but you can substitute the finely chopped zest of half a lemon. This recipe is easy to cook in larger quantities, and boiled rice is the right accompaniment.

Preheat the oven to 190°C/375°F/gas5 – allow 5 minutes for this before you start.

Peel the shallots and cut them into 2 or 3 pieces. Lightly crush the garlic cloves to loosen the skin and discard it. Trim the lemon grass, discarding tough outer leaves and cut the stems into 2 or 3 pieces.

Put the shallots, garlic, lemon grass, nuts, turmeric, coriander, chilli and half the oil in a food processor and work them to a purée.

Put the remaining oil in a sauté pan or shallow flameproof casserole — it should be large enough to hold all the chicken pieces touching the bottom so they cook evenly, covered in the sauce.

While you wait for the oil to heat, open the coconut milk. Add the puréed seasonings and spices to the hot oil and cook, stirring constantly, for 1-2 minutes. This mellows the flavour of the spices, but be careful not to let them toast.

Add the chicken pieces, skin-side down, and cook them for 2-3 minutes, turning once or twice to make sure they are well coated with seasonings. They will turn bright yellow from the turmeric.

Pour in the coconut milk and bring back to the boil. Cover the pan and cook in the preheated oven for 40-50 minutes, until the chicken pieces are very tender and fall easily from the prongs if you poke them with a carving fork. Once you've done this test once or twice you will quickly get to feel the difference between meat that is underdone and fully cooked.

At the end of cooking, the sauce should be quite thick and rich. If it has reduced too much the oil may have separated; if so, stir in half a cup of warm water and you'll find it will re-emulsify. Season the sauce to taste.

Serve the chicken from the casserole or transfer it to a serving dish.

RECAP

1 PREHEAT OVEN TO 190°C/375°F/GAS5 – ALLOW 5 MINUTES FOR THIS BEFORE YOU START.

2 PEEL SHALLOTS AND CUT INTO 2-3 PIECES. PEEL GARLIC. TRIM LEMON GRASS, DISCARDING TOUGH OUTER LEAVES, AND CUT INTO 2-3 PIECES.

3 PURÉE SHALLOTS, GARLIC, LEMON GRASS, NUTS, TURMERIC, CORIANDER, CHILLI AND HALF THE OIL IN A FOOD PROCESSOR.

4 HEAT REMAINING OIL IN SAUTÉ PAN OR SHALLOW FLAMEPROOF CASSEROLE. ADD VEGETABLE MIXTURE AND FRY, STIRRING CONSTANTLY, 1-2 MINUTES. ADD CHICKEN AND COOK 2-3 MINUTES, TURNING OCCASIONALLY.

5 STIR IN COCONUT MILK AND BRING BACK TO BOIL. COVER PAN AND COOK IN OVEN 40-50 MINUTES, UNTIL CHICKEN PIECES ARE VERY TENDER WHEN PIERCED WITH FORK. SEASON SAUCE TO TASTE.

6 SERVE FROM CASSEROLE OR TRANSFER TO SERVING DISH.

TAJINE OF CHICKEN WITH AUBERGINE

TIME IN KITCHEN
14 minutes
SIMMERING *1-1¼ hours*
STORAGE *up to 2 days in the refrigerator*

serves 4

I had never simmered a whole dish in earthenware until I bought a picturesque Moroccan tajine, *with its tall conical lid and base which doubles as a serving dish. The gentle even spread of heat works wonders in blending flavours and now I'm an addict. Even better,* tajine *recipes tend to look after themselves once you've layered the ingredients. The dish is always used on the hob (few Moroccan homes are equipped with ovens — in fact, bread doughs are taken daily to the local baker to be cooked in the communal oven). If you can't find a* tajine, *don't worry as a small round flameproof casserole works perfectly — it should be almost filled by the chicken and aubergine.*

Saffron adds glowing colour and aroma to this dish, but here is one occasion where less expensive powdered saffron is as good as the threads. Or, for a total change of pace, you can substitute ground cinnamon for the saffron, allowing two teaspoonfuls. Any tajine *reheats well; simply refrigerate it in the cooking pot and reheat it on the hob. Couscous or boiled rice is the appropriate accompaniment.*

1.8 kg / 4 lb oven-ready chicken, cut into 8 pieces
2 medium aubergines (about 750 g / 1½ lb in total)
1 garlic clove
1 teaspoon ground ginger
large pinch of saffron
1 teaspoon salt, or more to taste
4 tablespoons olive oil
2 large onions
1 lemon
freshly ground black pepper

tajine or small round flameproof casserole with a lid (about 22.5 cm / 9 in across)

Preheat the grill — allow 5 minutes for this before you begin the recipe.

Trim the aubergines, cut them across into 1.25 cm / ½ in slices. Set these on an oven rack and sprinkle with salt and pepper. Many recipes call for salting of the aubergine to draw out the juices but here we don't have time and I've found that grilling makes it unnecessary.

Put the aubergine slices quite close to the grill, about 5 cm / 2 in from the heat.

Meanwhile, lightly crush the garlic with the flat of a knife to loosen and remove the skin. Crush the clove, then chop it with the knife blade. Mix the garlic, ginger, saffron, salt and oil in a small bowl.

Arrange the chicken pieces in the tajine or casserole — it should be large enough for them all to touch the bottom. Spoon over half of the spice mixture, cover and set the pot over medium heat. You'll find that a tajine takes quite a while to heat, and if you are using it over a gas flame, it's wise to protect the tajine with a heat spreader.

Keep an eye on the grilling aubergine and turn the slices after 5-6 minutes, as soon as they brown. Leave them to brown on the other side for another 5-6 minutes. The more they dry, the better.

Peel the onions, leaving a little of the root to hold them together for slicing. Cut them in half through root and stem and thinly slice them.

Remove the lid and spread the onions over the chicken. Top with the browned aubergine. The pot will seem very full, but the vegetables will shrink as they cook. Spoon over the remaining spice mixture, cover and continue cooking over a low heat for 1 hour.

Squeeze the juice from the lemon and reserve it.

Test the chicken with a carving fork — it should be very tender and fall easily from the prongs. However, cooking time varies very much depending on the heat and thickness of your pot, so you may need to continue cooking 15 minutes, or even 30.

When the chicken is tender, transfer the pieces to a plate. The vegetables will be cooked down to a savoury pulp. Pour over the lemon juice, stir well and adjust seasoning. Replace the chicken on the vegetables and serve very hot from the cooking pot.

RECAP

1 PREHEAT GRILL — ALLOW 5 MINUTES FOR THIS BEFORE YOU START.

2 TRIM AUBERGINES, CUT ACROSS INTO 1.25 CM / ½ IN SLICES. SET ON OVEN RACK AND SPRINKLE WITH SALT AND PEPPER. GRILL CLOSE TO HEAT UNTIL BROWNED AND QUITE DRY, 5-6 MINUTES EACH SIDE.

3 MEANWHILE, CHOP GARLIC AND MIX IN SMALL BOWL WITH GINGER, SAFFRON, SALT AND OIL.

4 ARRANGE CHICKEN PIECES IN TAJINE OR CASSEROLE AND SPOON OVER HALF SPICE MIXTURE. COVER AND SET OVER MEDIUM HEAT.

5 PEEL AND SLICE ONIONS. SPREAD OVER CHICKEN AND TOP WITH BROWNED AUBERGINE. SPOON OVER REMAINING SPICE MIXTURE. COVER AND CONTINUE COOKING OVER LOW HEAT FOR 1 HOUR. SQUEEZE LEMON JUICE AND RESERVE IT.

6 TEST CHICKEN WITH FORK; IT SHOULD BE VERY TENDER. IF NOT, CONTINUE COOKING 15-30 MINUTES. TRANSFER PIECES TO PLATE. POUR LEMON JUICE OVER VEGETABLES, STIR WELL AND TASTE. REPLACE CHICKEN ON VEGETABLES AND SERVE.

DEVILLED CRAB SOUFFLÉ

TIME IN KITCHEN
11 minutes
STANDING up to 2 hours
in the refrigerator
before baking
BAKING 20-25 minutes

serves 4

When we lived in Washington D.C., one of the great treats of summer was freshly cleaned crab meat from the Chesapeake Bay. It was expensive, so I soon learned to make it go further in this soufflé, which is based on a popular Eastern Shore recipe for devilled crab meat. Fresh crab meat is certainly the best (try to find it unpasteurized for maximum flavour), but good canned crab is more than acceptable.

For maximum effect, the soufflé is baked in one large dish. If you are in a real hurry, I'd suggest you bake the mixture in individual ramekins as they will take only 10-12 minutes. It is a myth, by the way, that a soufflé must be baked immediately once the whites have been added. A mixture like this, thickened with flour, can be left in the refrigerator up to 2 hours before baking. Once in the oven, however, the countdown to the table is as tight as a satellite launch — just time to dress a green salad as an accompaniment!

Preheat the oven to 190°C/375°F/gas5, allowing at least 5 minutes before beginning the recipe for this. Make sure to set the shelf down low in the oven.

Butter the soufflé dish, taking care to coat the edges thoroughly so the soufflé rises evenly without sticking.

Make a white sauce: melt the butter in a medium saucepan, whisk in the flour and stir until foaming. Add the cream and heat, stirring constantly, until the sauce boils and thickens. Simmer, stirring constantly, for 30 seconds so the flour is thoroughly cooked. Take the pan from the heat, stir in the mustard, Worcestershire sauce, Tabasco, salt and pepper and set the sauce aside.

Separate the eggs, dropping the egg yolks into the sauce and the whites into the bowl of your mixer. Add the 3 extra whites with a pinch of salt and set the mixer going at medium-high speed to whisk the whites until stiff.

375 g / ¾ lb crab meat
30 g / 1 oz butter
15 g / ½ oz flour
250 ml / 8 fl oz single
    cream
1 teaspoon dry
    mustard, or more to
    taste
4 tablespoons
    Worcestershire
    sauce, or more to
    taste
2 teaspoons Tabasco
    sauce, or more to
    taste
salt and pepper
2 eggs, plus whites of
    3 more eggs

*1.5 litre / 2⅓ pt soufflé
    dish or 4 ramekins*
food mixer

Meanwhile, stir the egg yolks into the sauce – the heat of the sauce will cook and thicken them slightly. With your fingers, flake the crab meat into the sauce, picking out any membrane as you go. Stir and adjust the seasoning, adding more Tabasco, salt and pepper to taste. The mixture should be quite highly seasoned to balance the bland egg whites.

By now the egg whites should be stiff. Add about a quarter of them to the crab meat mixture and fold them in very thoroughly – this lightens the mixture and makes it easier to fold into the remaining whites. Tip the mixture into the remaining whites and fold them together as lightly as possible – this is the key to a light soufflé. However, if they get over-folded, don't worry: the soufflé will rise less but will still taste delicious. In fact, if you would prefer to make devilled crab in the first place, simply leave out the egg whites and bake the crab meat mixture in ramekins.

Transfer the crab meat mixture to the soufflé dish – it should fill it to within 1 cm / ½ in of the rim. Smooth the top with a metal spatula and run your thumb around the edge of the dish. This helps the soufflé rise evenly. At this stage you can keep the soufflé for up to 2 hours in the refrigerator.

Set the dish on a baking sheet and bake in the preheated oven for 20-25 minutes, until the soufflé is puffed and brown. When you shake the dish lightly, the mixture should be firm around the edge but still slightly wobbly in the centre.

Alert your guests to be ready at table. Transfer the soufflé to a large plate lined with a napkin (so the dish cannot slip) and bear it at once to the table. Use 2 spoons for serving, hollowing well into the centre so each person receives some of the brown outside and softer centre.

RECAP

1 *PREHEAT OVEN TO 190°C/375°F/GAS5 AND SET SHELF LOW. ALLOW 5 MINUTES FOR OVEN TO HEAT UP BEFORE BEGINNING. BUTTER SOUFFLÉ DISH.*

2 *MAKE WHITE SAUCE WITH BUTTER, FLOUR AND CREAM, SIMMERING 30 SECONDS. TAKE FROM HEAT AND STIR IN MUSTARD, WORCESTERSHIRE SAUCE, TABASCO, SALT AND PEPPER. SET SAUCE ASIDE.*

3 *SEPARATE EGGS AND STIR YOLKS INTO SAUCE. ADD PINCH OF SALT TO WHITES AND STIFFLY WHISK IN ELECTRIC MIXER.*

4 *MEANWHILE, PICK OVER CRAB MEAT, STIR INTO WHITE SAUCE AND SEASON QUITE HIGHLY TO TASTE.*

5 *ADD ABOUT ONE-QUARTER OF WHIPPED EGG WHITES TO CRAB MEAT MIXTURE AND FOLD TOGETHER THOROUGHLY. ADD THIS TO REMAINING WHITES AND FOLD TOGETHER AS LIGHTLY AS POSSIBLE.*

6 *TRANSFER TO SOUFFLÉ DISH, SMOOTH TOP WITH METAL SPATULA AND RUN THUMB AROUND EDGE.*

7 *BAKE SOUFFLÉ IN PREHEATED OVEN 20-25 MINUTES, UNTIL PUFFED AND BROWN. WHEN SHAKEN, CENTRE SHOULD BE SLIGHTLY SOFT.*

8 *TRANSFER DISH TO NAPKIN-LINED PLATE AND SERVE AT ONCE.*

BRETON CHAUDRÉE

TIME IN KITCHEN
13 minutes
SIMMERING *6-8 minutes*

serves 4

500 g / 1 lb cod fillets
1 dozen washed
mussels
500 g / 1 lb red
potatoes
500 ml / 16 fl oz double
cream
500 ml / 16 fl oz milk
250 ml / 8 fl oz bottled
clam juice
1 bay leaf
30 g / 1 oz butter
2 onions
salt and freshly ground
black pepper

The ancestor of New England chowder is 'chaudrée', the creation of Breton fishermen who cooked up unsold or damaged fish with milk and potatoes, topping the pot with mussels for flavour. You'll still find it in the little ports along the coast of Brittany. I like to use the traditional cod, but you can substitute any robust white fish, or even scallops. For a full meal, add croûtes of French bread, brushed with butter and browned in the oven.

Put a medium pan of salted water on to heat, cover and bring it to the boil. Allow 5 minutes for this before you start the recipe.

Wash the potatoes and cut them into 1.25 cm / ½ in dice, leaving the skins on. When the water is boiling, add the diced potato. Cover and bring back to the boil. Simmer for 8-10 minutes, until just tender when poked with a knife. This speeds cooking time as potatoes (and all roots) cook more quickly in water than in milk.

Put the cream, milk, clam juice and bay leaf in a separate pan to warm over a low heat. Melt the butter in a large soup pan over a low heat.

Meanwhile, peel the onions, leaving a little of the root. Cut them in half from stem to root and set the halves cut side down on the cutting board. Thinly slice them, again cutting from stem to root. Stir the onion into the butter and leave over a low heat.

Wash the fish in cold water and dry on paper towels. Cut them into 2.5 cm / 1 in cubes. If you need to clean the mussels, scrub them with a wire brush under cold running water to remove the barnacles and pull their stringy 'beards' from the shells with a knife. Discard any open mussels that do not close when tapped as they may be dead.

When the potatoes are tender, drain them in a colander and add to the onion with some pepper. Salt may not be needed as the clam juice and mussels are already salty. Stir the hot milk mixture into the potatoes and bring just to the boil. Taste and adjust the seasoning, if necessary. Simmer for 2 minutes to let the flavours blend. Don't cover the pan as it is more likely to boil over, and be sure it cooks only at a low simmer.

Stir the cod into the chowder and set the mussels on top. Cover and simmer for 6-8 minutes longer, until the mussels steam open and the cod just flakes easily. Discard the bay leaf. Taste and adjust the seasoning if necessary. Serve at once, spooning the chowder over French bread croûtes, if you like.

RECAP

1 PUT MEDIUM PAN OF SALTED WATER TO HEAT, COVER AND BRING TO BOIL. ALLOW 5 MINUTES FOR THIS BEFORE STARTING.

2 WASH POTATOES AND CUT INTO 1.25 CM / ½ IN DICE, LEAVING SKINS. ADD TO BOILING WATER AND SIMMER 8-10 MINUTES, UNTIL JUST TENDER.

3 MEANWHILE, GENTLY WARM MILK, CREAM, CLAM JUICE AND BAY LEAF IN SEPARATE PAN.

4 MELT BUTTER IN LARGE PAN. PEEL AND SLICE ONION, STIR INTO BUTTER AND SOFTEN OVER LOW HEAT.

5 WASH AND DRY FISH FILLETS. CUT INTO 2.5 CM / 1 IN CUBES. CLEAN MUSSELS, IF NECESSARY.

6 DRAIN POTATOES AND ADD TO PAN. STIR IN HOT MILK MIXTURE AND ADJUST SEASONING. SIMMER 2 MINUTES.

7 STIR IN COD, TOP WITH MUSSELS, COVER AND SIMMER 6-8 MINUTES UNTIL MUSSELS STEAM OPEN AND FISH FLAKES EASILY. DISCARD BAY LEAF AND ADJUST SEASONING AGAIN.

8 SERVE AT ONCE.

BAKED SCALLOPS WITH HERB BUTTER

TIME IN KITCHEN
11 minutes
BAKING *15-20 minutes*
   (5-6 in the microwave)

serves 4

750 g / 1½ lb shelled
   scallops
90 g / 3 oz unsalted
   butter
2 shallots
small bunch of chervil
small bunch of
   tarragon
small bunch of chives
2 tablespoons white
   wine
salt and freshly ground
   black pepper

*4 heatproof dishes with
lids or 4 large
ramekins*

This simple little recipe is a perfect balance of sweet scallops, piquant shallot and fragrant 'fines herbes' – the classic mix of chervil, tarragon and chives – all moistened with a touch of butter. The scallops are baked in little dishes – I have some with lids – but large ramekins tightly covered with foil are just as effective. To enjoy the full aroma when the lid is lifted, take the dishes covered to the table. Parsley can replace chervil and you can use smaller queen scallops, though they can lack the sweetness of the larger sea scallops.

This recipe is easy to double or triple and you can shorten baking time by using the microwave. Serve it with something to absorb the buttery scallop juices – little boiled potatoes in their jackets or simply some crusty bread – and a fragrant white wine.

Preheat the oven to 230°C/450°F/gas8 – allow 5-10 minutes for this before you start.

Drain any juice from the scallops – if they are swimming in liquid it is a sign they were frozen and will have lost flavour. Discard the small crescent-shaped membrane from the side of the scallops as it is very tough. Divide them among the baking dishes or ramekins – they should all touch the bottom so they cook evenly.

Melt the butter over a very low heat in a medium saucepan or in the microwave.

Meanwhile, peel the shallots, leaving a bit of the root to hold them together. If they do not have a flat side, cut them in half and set flat side down on the board. Slice them as thinly as possible, add to the butter and leave to sauté over a medium heat. Alternatively, cook them for 4 minutes in the microwave on high.

Strip the chervil and tarragon leaves from the stems and chop the leaves, taking care not to chop too finely as they bruise easily. Add them to the butter. With scissors, snip the chives into the butter. Stir in the white wine. Take from the heat and add a little salt and generous amounts of pepper. Stir and spoon the mixture over the scallops.

Add lids to the dishes or cover ramekins tightly with foil. Set on a baking sheet and bake for 15-20 minutes: the time will vary according to the thickness of the dishes.

If using the microwave, cover the dishes with microwave film, set them on the turntable and cook for 5-6 minutes on high.

Lift one lid: if steam has bubbled to touch the lid, the scallops are done. Serve them at once as they become tough and dry if overcooked.

RECAP

1 PREHEAT OVEN TO 230°C/450°F/GAS8 – ALLOW 5-10 MINUTES FOR THIS BEFORE YOU BEGIN.

2 DRAIN ANY JUICES FROM SCALLOPS AND DISCARD CRESCENT-SHAPED MEMBRANE FROM SIDES. DIVIDE AMONG BAKING DISHES.

3 MELT BUTTER OVER LOW HEAT, OR IN MICROWAVE.

4 MEANWHILE, CHOP SHALLOTS AND LEAVE TO SAUTÉ IN BUTTER OR COOK ABOUT 4 MINUTES IN MICROWAVE.

5 CHOP CHERVIL AND TARRAGON AND ADD TO BUTTER. WITH SCISSORS, SNIP CHIVES INTO BUTTER. STIR IN WHITE WINE.

6 TAKE FROM HEAT AND SEASON. STIR AND SPOON MIXTURE OVER SCALLOPS.

7 COVER DISHES, IF NECESSARY MAKING LIDS WITH FOIL OR MICROWAVE FILM. SET ON BAKING SHEET AND BAKE 15-20 MINUTES. (IN MICROWAVE, SET ON TURNTABLE AND ALLOW 5-6 MINUTES ON HIGH.) LIFT ONE LID: IF STEAM HAS BUBBLED TO TOUCH LID, SCALLOPS ARE READY. SERVE AT ONCE.

SNAPPER WITH GREEN OLIVE TAPENADE

TIME IN KITCHEN
10 minutes
BAKING *12-15 minutes*
(6 in the microwave)

serves 4

I came across green olive tapenade when staying with author and restaurant critic Patricia Wells in her home in Provence. We both enjoyed its gentle flavour and crunch of almond, so back home I made haste to recreate it.

Be sure to buy thick fillets of a robust fish, such as red snapper, halibut or cod. After baking with the tapenade, the fish becomes deliciously perfumed with olives and salt. Look for large, meaty green olives — good ones come from Spain — already stoned to save you time. To save even more time, you can cook the fish in the microwave. As an accompaniment I'd suggest the Provençal Tricolor (page 103) or simply some roasted sweet peppers.

500 g / 1 lb red snapper
  fillets
olive oil for brushing
1 lemon

for the tapenade:
1 slice of white bread
2 garlic cloves
75 g / 2½ oz stoned
  green olives
2 anchovy fillets
30 g / 1 oz flaked
  almonds
2 tablespoons capers
4 tablespoons olive oil
freshly ground black
  pepper

food processor

Preheat the oven to 190°C/375°F/gas5 – allow 5 minutes for this before you start.

Pour 125 ml / 4 fl oz cold water over the bread for the tapenade in a small bowl and leave it to soak – for a lighter, less pungent tapenade, you can add more bread.

Brush the baking dish with a little olive oil. Rinse the fish fillets in cold water, dry them and cut into 4 equal pieces. Set them in the baking dish. Cut 4 slices from the lemon and set the rest aside.

Prepare the tapenade: lightly crush the garlic cloves and discard the skin. Put them in the food processor with the olives, anchovy fillets and almonds. Drain the capers in a strainer, rinse them under cold water and add to the olives. Squeeze the bread in your hands to extract the water and add the bread to the processor.

Using the pulse button, coarsely chop the ingredients. Then, with the blades turning, gradually pour in the oil so the tapenade is puréed to a smooth, slightly stiff sauce.

Work in the juice from the reserved lemon half together with plenty of pepper. Taste the tapenade, adding more lemon juice and pepper to taste – it is unlikely to need salt as the olives and anchovy are already salty.

Spoon some tapenade on each piece of fish and top with a slice of lemon. Bake the fish in the preheated oven for 12-15 minutes, until it just flakes easily when tested with a fork. If you like fish lightly done, take it from the oven when a thin translucent line remains in the centre.

If you want to save time and use the microwave, set the fish with its topping in a microwave dish and cover tightly with microwave film. Cook for 5-6 minutes on high.

Serve it from the baking dish while still hot.

RECAP

1 PREHEAT OVEN TO 190°C/375°F/GAS5 – ALLOW 5 MINUTES FOR THIS BEFORE STARTING.

2 SOAK BREAD IN 125 ML / 4 FL OZ COLD WATER. OIL BAKING DISH. WASH AND DRY FISH FILLETS. CUT INTO 4 PIECES AND LAY IN DISH. CUT 4 SLICES FROM LEMON AND SET ASIDE REST.

3 PEEL GARLIC AND PUT IN PROCESSOR WITH OLIVES, ANCHOVIES, ALMONDS AND DRAINED RINSED CAPERS. SQUEEZE BREAD DRY AND ADD. PULSE TO COARSELY CHOP, THEN GRADUALLY ADD OIL, WITH MACHINE TURNING. WORK IN JUICE OF RESERVED HALF LEMON WITH PLENTY OF PEPPER. TASTE AND ADD MORE LEMON AND PEPPER IF NEEDED.

4 SPOON TAPENADE ON FISH AND TOP WITH LEMON SLICE. BAKE FOR 12-15 MINUTES, UNTIL FISH FLAKES EASILY WHEN FORKED. SERVE HOT.

* IF USING MICROWAVE, SET FISH IN A MICROWAVE DISH AND COVER TIGHTLY WITH MICROWAVE FILM. COOK 5-6 MINUTES ON HIGH.

MONKFISH WITH PANCETTA & SPINACH

TIME IN KITCHEN
11 minutes
ROASTING *25-30 minutes*
(15-18 in the microwave)

serves 4

Monkfish is an excellent example of fashion. Escoffier wouldn't touch it unless heavily disguised in a tomato 'sauce américaine', but monkfish is today's darling, prized for its firm white flesh and lack of bones. Most of it is farmed, guaranteeing fillets of a handy 375 g / ¾ lb size, with a sweet mild flavour. I like to pep it up a bit by wrapping the fillets in Italian pancetta, or plain smoked streaky bacon if pancetta is scarce. The roast also does well in the microwave and you can save about 15 minutes' cooking time.

Monkfish fillets have a curious membrane under the skin which must be removed before cooking. If this has not been done at the fish counter, before you start you'll need to spend an extra few minutes cutting it away with a sharp knife. Pancetta is much easier to handle when it is cold, so you may want to chill it before you begin.

Of course, the monkfish fillets can vary very much in size: if they are small, just pile them up on top of each other; if you only have one large fillet, fold it over on itself to give the required 'roast of meat' effect.

about 750 g / 1½ lb monkfish fillets
250 g / ½ lb sliced pancetta
1 tablespoon olive oil
45 g / 1½ oz butter
1 onion
1 kg / 2 lb washed spinach
½ lemon
½ teaspoon freshly grated nutmeg
salt and freshly ground black pepper

Preheat the oven to 190°C/375°F/gas5 – allow 5 minutes for this before you begin.

Wash the monkfish fillets and dry them on paper towels.

Spread the pancetta slices on the work surface in an overlapping line about 10 cm / 4 in longer than the monkfish fillets. Set the fillets head to tail on top of the pancetta to form a cylinder as long as the longest fillet. Bring up the pancetta around them. or, if the slices are short, cover with another layer of pancetta slices and tie up the package with string like a joint of meat.

Add the oil to the roasting pan. Sprinkle the fish roast on both sides with salt and pepper and set it in the roasting pan. Bake in the oven for 25-30 minutes. If using the microwave, set the roast in a microwave dish, cover tightly with microwave film and cook 15-18 minutes at high.

Gently heat the butter in a sauté pan or deep frying pan. Meanwhile peel the onion, leaving a little of the root. Cut it in half from the stem to root and set the halves cut side down on the board. Very thinly slice them and add to the pan with a little salt and pepper. Sauté over medium heat until soft.

Meanwhile, remove the stems from the spinach: fold each leaf in half and pull away the stem, leaving the soft leaves. Add the leaves to the onion with salt and pepper and toss over the heat for 1-2 minutes until wilted. The salt will help them wilt faster.

Squeeze the juice from the lemon half over the spinach. Sprinkle it with nutmeg, add more salt and pepper to taste and set aside.

To see if the roast is cooked insert a skewer into the centre of the fish just as you would a roast of meat. Leave it for 30 seconds to absorb the heat. Pull it out and press it to your wrist; it should be very hot, showing the centre of the fish is cooked. If cool or warm, it is not yet done. When the roast is ready, transfer it to a carving board.

Put the wilted spinach in the roasting pan, stir and return it to the oven to reheat. In the microwave, allow 45-60 seconds on high.

Meanwhile, carve the roast into thick slices, discarding the strings. You will find that the gelatine in the fish holds the fillets together in tidy slices. Arrange the monkfish slices on a warmed serving dish or 4 individual plates and pile the spinach beside them.

RECAP

1 PREHEAT OVEN TO 190°C/375°F/GAS 5 – ALLOW 5 MINUTES FOR THIS BEFORE YOU BEGIN.

2 RINSE AND DRY FISH. SPREAD PANCETTA SLICES IN OVERLAPPING LINE ON WORK SURFACE AND SET FILLETS ON TOP, HEAD TO TAIL. WRAP PANCETTA ROUND FISH OR TOP WITH ANOTHER LAYER AND TIE UP LIKE MEAT JOINT.

3 BAKE IN PAN BRUSHED WITH OIL FOR 25-30 MINUTES, OR TIGHTLY COVER WITH MICROWAVE FILM AND MICROWAVE 15-18 MINUTES ON HIGH.

4 HEAT BUTTER IN SAUTÉ PAN UNTIL FOAMING. CUT ONION INTO SMALL DICE. ADD TO PAN WITH SALT AND PEPPER AND COOK UNTIL SOFTENED.

5 MEANWHILE, PULL STEMS FROM SPINACH AND ADD LEAVES TO ONION, TOSSING OVER HEAT UNTIL WILTED. ADD JUICE FROM HALF LEMON, WITH NUTMEG AND MORE SALT AND PEPPER IF NECESSARY.

6 THE FISH IS DONE WHEN SKEWER INSERTED IN CENTRE IS HOT TO TOUCH WHEN WITHDRAWN AFTER 30 SECONDS. WHEN COOKED, TRANSFER TO CARVING BOARD AND CUT IN THICK SLICES, DISCARDING STRINGS.

7 ADD SPINACH TO ROASTING PAN AND PUT BACK IN OVEN TO REHEAT, OR HEAT 45-60 SECONDS IN MICROWAVE.

8 ARRANGE SLICES OF MONKFISH ROAST ON WARMED PLATTER OR INDIVIDUAL PLATES AND PILE SPINACH BESIDE THEM.

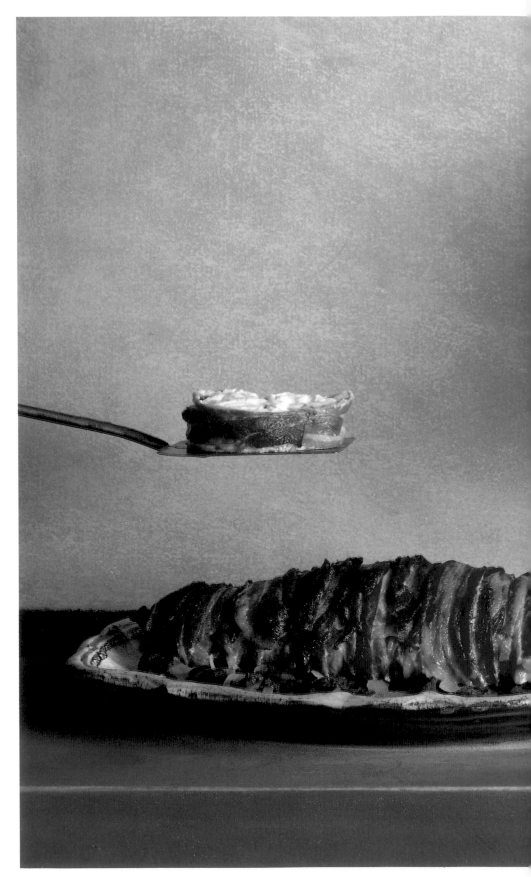

TROUT WITH FENNEL
& HERBS EN PAPILLOTE

TIME IN KITCHEN
   14 minutes
STANDING *up to 4 hours*
   in the refrigerator
   before baking
BAKING *25-35 minutes*
   (4-6 in the microwave
   for 2 papillotes)

serves 4

4 trout fillets (each
   about 175 g / 6 oz)
2 medium fennel bulbs
75 g / 2½ oz butter
1 medium bunch of
   dill
4 tablespoons Pernod
   or other aniseed-
   flavoured liquor
salt and freshly ground
   black pepper

4 sheets of greaseproof
   paper, each about
   30 x 40 cm / 12 x 16 in

Cooking in paper is nothing new. A medieval cookbook advises protecting delicate meats from the flames of an open fire by wrapping them in oiled paper (an expensive remedy for the times). At the turn of the last century, Nicholas Soyer wrote a whole book entitled Paper Bag Cookery. *He claimed that the atmosphere created within the paper bag would 'impart a wholesome fullness to the food that constitutes ... a new and delicious effect.'*

Now dignified by the French term of 'en papillote', paper-bag cookery enables a whole main course to be cooked together in an elegant individual parcel of greaseproof paper. Little or no fat is needed as all the cooking juices are retained inside the parcel. Fish does particularly well en papillote, *whether it's salmon, sea bass or trout as I suggest here. The parcel browns and puffs with steam, looking both pretty and telling you when the food is ready. Please don't be tempted to substitute foil, which will do neither.*

The aroma when a papillote is broken open at the table is half the charm of the dish. Even better, you can prepare the parcels up to 4 hours ahead and bake them just before serving — the only limit to numbers is the size of your oven. If you're cooking for two, you can save time by using the microwave, but there is not room for more than 2 parcels.

Preheat the oven to 190°C/375°F/gas5 – allow 5 minutes for this before you start.

Trim the stems and roots of the fennel bulbs and cut them in half from stem to root. Set the halves cut side down on a board and slice them very thinly, working from stem to root. The thinner the slices, the more quickly they will cook.

Melt half the butter in a frying pan. Add the fennel with salt and pepper to taste and press a piece of foil on top. Leave to cook over a high heat for 3-4 minutes, stirring occasionally, until the fennel has absorbed most of the butter and is softer but still crisp.

Meanwhile, melt the remaining butter in a small pan or warm it in the microwave.

To shape the papillotes, fold in half lengthwise each of the 4 sheets of greaseproof paper and open them out again. Dip a brush in the melted butter and brush the papers. This prevents them from scorching in the heat of the oven.

Rinse the trout fillets with cold water and dry them on paper towels. Strip the dill leaves from all but 4 of the stems and coarsely chop the leaves. Stir the chopped dill into the fennel and adjust the seasoning, if necessary.

Spread the fennel in a bed to one side of the fold on each piece of paper, making it about the same size as a trout fillet. Set a fillet on top, skin side up if your fish has a pretty skin. Sprinkle with salt, pepper and Pernod. Top with a dill sprig. Fold the paper back over the trout and press the edges together. Starting at one side of the fold, pleat the paper on itself to seal the edges, working around to finish again at the fold.

Transfer the parcels to a baking sheet and bake in the preheated oven for 25-35 minutes, until they are puffed up and brown. When cooked, steam from the food will puff the paper into a balloon. Alternatively, set only 2 packages on the turntable of the microwave and cook for 4-6 minutes on high.

Transfer the parcels to warmed plates and serve at once, as they deflate rapidly. In a restaurant, the waiter would snip open the case, so you may want to provide a pair of scissors so each person has the pleasure of opening their own surprise package.

RECAP

1 PREHEAT OVEN TO 190°C/375°F/GAS5. TRIM FENNEL, CUT IN HALVES AND SLICE VERY THINLY.

2 MELT HALF BUTTER IN FRYING PAN, ADD FENNEL, SALT AND PEPPER AND PRESS FOIL ON TOP. LEAVE TO COOK OVER HIGH HEAT FOR 3-4 MINUTES, UNTIL FENNEL IS SLIGHTLY SOFT.

3 MELT REMAINING BUTTER. FOLD 4 LARGE PIECES OF GREASEPROOF PAPER IN HALF. OPEN AND BRUSH WITH MELTED BUTTER.

4 RINSE AND DRY TROUT. STRIP DILL LEAVES FROM ALL BUT 4 STEMS AND COARSELY CHOP. STIR CHOPPED DILL INTO FENNEL AND ADJUST SEASONING.

5 SPREAD FENNEL IN A BED ON EACH PAPER, SET A FILLET ON TOP AND SPRINKLE WITH SALT, PEPPER AND PERNOD. TOP EACH FILLET WITH SPRIG OF DILL. FOLD PAPER OVER TROUT AND PLEAT EDGES TO SEAL.

6 TRANSFER TO BAKING SHEET AND BAKE FOR 25-35 MINUTES, UNTIL PUFFED AND BROWN. ALTERNATIVELY, COOK 2 CASES IN MICROWAVE FOR 4-6 MINUTES ON HIGH.

7 TRANSFER TO WARMED PLATES AND SERVE AT ONCE.

ROAST FISH BELLE FLORENCE

TIME IN KITCHEN
12 minutes
ROASTING *30-35 minutes*

serves 4

There's a lot to say about this recipe. Let's start with the fish: salmon, bream and sea bass are particularly good for roasting, but don't overlook more modest hake or trout. For speed I'm suggesting one large fish to serve four people, roasting it for 30-35 minutes. Don't worry if it's a bit big as leftovers are delicious in salad. You can also substitute two smaller fish of about 750 g / 1½ lb each, roasting them for 25-30 minutes.

Preparation of the fish is important. If you don't want to spend time on the messy job of trimming and scaling, be sure it's done for you at the fish counter — the stomach cleaned, the gills removed, the fins trimmed and the tail cut in the traditional 'V'. If you have the head left on, so much the better — not only is presentation more impressive, but the eye of the cooked fish will help you judge when it is done.

The choice of ingredients to roast with the fish is up to you. You may want to substitute courgettes, peppers or fennel for the mushrooms in the main recipe; or go Oriental, with a touch of ginger and garlic instead of Mediterranean herbs, as in the variation. It's your call whether to serve this dish hot or cooled to room temperature.

As for the name, 'la belle Florence' was our receptionist at La Varenne cooking school, a woman of great charm and worthy inspiration of an outstanding dish.

1 whole fish (see above), weighing about 1.5 kg / 3½ lb, cleaned, scaled and trimmed
1 onion
4 tablespoons olive oil
500 g / 1 lb tomatoes
250 g / ½ lb mushrooms
1 tablespoon mixed dried Provençal herbs
1 lemon
4 sprigs of fresh thyme
salt and pepper

large flameproof roasting pan large enough to take the fish

Preheat the oven to 190°C/375°F/gas5 — allow 5 minutes for this before you start.

Peel the onion and cut it in half through stem and root. Set each half flat side down and slice very thinly — the thinner it is the more quickly it will cook.

Heat half the oil in the roasting pan. Add the onion, stir and leave to sauté over medium heat.

Meanwhile, cut the cores from the tomatoes and cut them across in 1 cm / ⅜ in slices. Trim the mushroom stems and wipe the caps with a damp cloth. If the mushrooms are sandy, drop them into a large bowl of cold water, stir them so the sand falls to the bottom and lift them out with your hands so the sand is left behind. Thickly slice them.

Add the tomatoes and mushrooms to the onions together with the Provençal herbs, salt and pepper. Stir to mix and leave to cook over medium heat.

Wash the fish, especially in the cavity, and pat it dry with paper towels. With a knife, diagonally slash each side of the fish 4 times so the heat can penetrate the flesh and cook the fish more evenly.

Cut two slices from the lemon and halve them. Insert a sprig of thyme and a lemon slice in each slash on the upper side of the fish. Remove the vegetables from the heat and set the fish on top. Squeeze the juice from the remaining lemon over the fish and drizzle it with the remaining olive oil. Sprinkle it with salt and pepper.

Cover the roasting pan with foil and roast in the oven for 30-35 minutes, until the fish flakes when tested with a fork and is opaque in the centre. When the fish is done, the eyes will turn white and pop up from the socket. Don't be tempted to try to save time by using the microwave as a dish of this size will cook unevenly.

Transfer the fish to a serving platter. Adjust the seasoning of the vegetables, if necessary, and spoon them around the fish. Serve hot, or allow the fish to cool to room temperature (about an hour).

ROAST FISH WITH CELERY & GINGER

Fresh ginger and lime juice are natural partners for fish, with celery adding a crunchy background.

In the recipe above, omit the onion, tomatoes, mushrooms, thyme and herbs. You will need 150 ml / ¼ pt olive oil as it is absorbed by the potatoes. Trim and cut a medium bunch of celery into 1 cm / ⅜ in slices. Wash the slices under cold running water in a colander.

Heat half the oil and sauté the celery as for the onion. Meanwhile peel and chop 2 garlic cloves and stir them into the celery with some salt and pepper. Slice a walnut-sized piece of fresh ginger, crush each slice and then chop them. Stir into the celery.

While they sauté, wash 4-5 potatoes and cut them into 1 cm / ⅜ in slices. Prepare the fish as described. Slice a lime as for the lemon and insert slices into the slashes in the fish.

Add the potatoes to the celery and toss to mix. Set the fish on top and sprinkle with the remaining olive oil, 125 ml / 4 fl oz white wine, the juice from the remaining half lime, salt and pepper. Cover the fish and roast it as described.

RECAP

1 PREHEAT OVEN TO 190°C/375°F/GAS5 – ALLOW 5 MINUTES FOR THIS BEFORE YOU BEGIN.

2 THINLY SLICE ONION. HEAT HALF OIL IN FLAMEPROOF ROASTING PAN, ADD ONION AND LEAVE TO SAUTÉ.

3 CORE AND THICKLY SLICE TOMATOES. TRIM MUSHROOM STEMS, WIPE CAPS AND THICKLY SLICE. ADD TOMATOES AND MUSHROOMS TO ONIONS WITH PROVENÇAL HERBS, SALT AND PEPPER. STIR TO MIX AND LEAVE TO COOK OVER MEDIUM HEAT.

4 WASH FISH, DRY AND SLASH EACH SIDE DIAGONALLY 4 TIMES. CUT 2 SLICES FROM LEMON AND HALVE THESE. INSERT SPRIG OF THYME AND LEMON HALF-SLICE IN EACH SLASH ON UPPER SIDE OF FISH.

5 TAKE VEGETABLES FROM HEAT AND SET FISH ON TOP. SQUEEZE JUICE FROM REMAINING LEMON OVER FISH AND DRIZZLE WITH REMAINING OIL. SEASON.

6 COVER ROASTING PAN WITH FOIL AND ROAST UNTIL FISH FLAKES WHEN FORKED AND IS OPAQUE IN CENTRE, 30-35 MINUTES.

7 TRANSFER FISH TO PLATTER. ADJUST SEASONING OF VEGETABLES AND SPOON AROUND FISH. SERVE HOT OR AT ROOM TEMPERATURE.

PORK CHOP WITH A CONFIT OF ONIONS

TIME IN KITCHEN
  13 minutes
SIMMERING
  30-35 minutes
STORAGE *(for the confit)*
  a week in the
  refrigerator
serves 4

4 pork chops
  (about 750 g / 1½ lb
  in total)
125 g / 4 oz butter
6-8 Spanish onions
  (about 1.4 kg / 3 lb)
250 ml / 8 fl oz red
  wine
1 tablespoon sugar
salt and freshly ground
  pepper

Confit of onions is hard to resist, so I was determined to shorten the usual hour-long recipe to something manageable for after-work supper. It's all a question of getting a quick start by cooking the onions in generous amounts of butter, then leaving them to soften gently with red wine for colour and a touch of sugar for sweetness. Onion confit complements rich meats like duck as well as pork. The pork chops require very little attention, so all your time can be spent on chopping a plentiful supply of onions. Spanish onions have the most flavour and the larger they are, the quicker you can slice them. Add mashed potatoes or pasta and you have a feast.

Melt about one-quarter of the butter in a frying pan. Season the pork chops on both sides and add them to the butter when it is just starting to brown. Cook for 4-5 minutes over a medium heat.

Meanwhile, melt the remaining butter in a sauté pan or shallow casserole over a medium heat. Peel 1 onion, leaving a little of the root. Cut it in half from stem to root, set it cut side down on the board and thinly slice it. Stir into the butter. Continue peeling and slicing onions, adding them one by one to the pan and stirring well.

Turn the chops after you have sliced 1 or 2 onions. Turn down the heat and leave the chops to brown on the other side while you finish the onions.

When the last onion is added to the pan, turn up the heat and sauté them for 2 minutes, stirring often. They should be quite brown and wilted.

Check the chops: they should be browned and well cooked in the centre – if not, pearls of juice will still be popping up on top. Transfer them to a plate.

Stir the wine, sugar, salt and pepper into the onions and bring to a boil. Turn down the heat to low, press a piece of foil down on the onions and put the lid on. The onions must now simmer very slowly and gently until soft and melting.

After the onions have cooked for 30-35 minutes, stir and adjust the seasoning. They should be very brown and may have caught on the bottom of the pan. Don't worry – this produces delicious caramelized juices which are essential for flavouring the confit. If the onions have not browned well, cook for 1-2 minutes over a high heat to finish.

Set the chops on top, cover tightly and leave over a low heat for 5 minutes to warm through. Serve from the casserole or transfer to individual plates.

RECAP

1 MELT ONE-QUARTER OF BUTTER IN FRYING PAN. SEASON CHOPS. BROWN 4-5 MINUTES OVER MEDIUM HEAT ON BOTH SIDES.

2 MEANWHILE, HEAT REMAINING BUTTER IN A SAUTÉ PAN OR SHALLOW CASSEROLE. PEEL ONION, THINLY SLICE AND STIR IN. CONTINUE STIRRING IN SLICED ONIONS ONE BY ONE.

3 WHEN LAST ONION IS ADDED, TURN UP HEAT AND SAUTÉ FOR 2 MINUTES, STIRRING UNTIL SLIGHTLY BROWNED AND WILTED.

4 CHECK CHOPS: THEY SHOULD BE BROWNED AND WELL COOKED IN CENTRE. TRANSFER TO PLATE.

5 STIR WINE, SUGAR, SALT AND PEPPER INTO ONIONS

AND BRING TO BOIL. PRESS FOIL ON TOP, ADD LID AND COOK VERY GENTLY 30-35 MINUTES.

6 SET CHOPS ON TOP OF ONIONS, COVER TIGHTLY AND PUT OVER LOW HEAT FOR 5 MINUTES TO WARM.

7 SERVE FROM CASSEROLE, OR ON INDIVIDUAL PLATES.

ROAST PORK LOIN WITH BAKER'S POTATOES

TIME IN KITCHEN
14 minutes
ROASTING 45-60 minutes

serves 4

Roasting pork in milk is an old Italian trick, a way to keep the pork moist and at the same time create some delectable brown gravy. The milk separates as it cooks, so the gravy looks slightly curdled, but don't let that worry you — it tastes wonderful. I usually buy a boned rolled roast, then unroll and fill it with lots of garlic, olive oil and herbs so that in effect it bastes itself from the inside. Here I'm using sage and thyme as we have lots in the garden at home, but you could substitute other aromatics, such as rosemary or oregano.

Half the garlic and herbs go into a dish of thinly sliced potatoes, baked in the oven beside the pork. The roast is also delicious cold, served if you like with Panzanella (see page 74) or Quick Ratatouille (see page 91) instead of the baker's potatoes. This hearty dish will take almost any kind of red wine — why not venture farther afield with something from Australia or Chile?

1 kg / 2 lb boneless rolled pork loin roast
4 garlic cloves
medium bunch of sage
medium bunch of thyme
1 teaspoon salt, more for sprinkling
3 tablespoons olive oil
1 teaspoon black peppercorns
500 ml / 16 fl oz milk
freshly ground black pepper

for the baker's potatoes:
2 tablespoons oil
1 large onion
4 medium potatoes (about 1 kg / 2 lb)
500 ml / 16 fl oz veal or chicken stock, or more if needed

Preheat the oven to 200°C/400°F/gas6 – allow 5-10 minutes for this before you start.

Crush the garlic cloves with the flat of a knife to loosen the skin and discard it. Put them in the food processor. Strip the sage leaves from the stems and add to the garlic. Strip the thyme leaves and add them to the processor, together with the teaspoon of salt and 2 tablespoons of the olive oil. Crush the peppercorns under the base of a heavy pan and add to the other ingredients. Work them to a purée.

Discard any strings from the pork and if necessary trim excess fat. Unroll the meat and spread it with about two-thirds of the garlic and herb purée, leaving the rest in the processor bowl. Roll the pork up again and tie with string. There's no need to be very neat about this, the meat simply needs to be held together.

Add the remaining oil to a medium flameproof casserole and put over quite a high heat. Add the pork, sprinkle with salt and pepper and leave it to brown while you prepare the potatoes, turning it from time to time.

Prepare the potatoes: heat the oil in a shallow flameproof baking dish. Peel the onion, leaving a little of the root, and cut it in half from stem to root. Set it cut side down on the board and thinly slice it, again cutting from stem to root. Stir it into the oil and leave to sauté over a medium heat.

Wash the potatoes and wipe them dry. Change the blade in the processor to the one for slicing. Use the processor to slice the potatoes thinly, letting them fall into the remaining garlic and herb purée.

By now the onions should be soft. Add the potatoes to them, stir until well mixed and spread them flat. Pour over the stock – the potatoes should be almost, but not quite, covered with liquid.

Cover with foil and put on a low shelf in the preheated oven to bake, adding an upper shelf for the pork. At the end of cooking, the potatoes should be very tender and have absorbed most of the stock. They take 45-60 minutes, the same time as the pork.

Turn the pork browned side up and add the milk. Cover the casserole and cook in the oven for 45-60 minutes. I like pork to be very tender and well cooked, so I test it with a skewer which acts as an old-fashioned meat thermometer. Insert the skewer in the centre of the meat and leave it for 30 seconds to absorb the heat. Pull it out and touch it to your wrist; it should be very hot, showing the centre of the meat is cooked.

*food processor with
chopping and slicing
blades
medium flameproof
casserole
shallow flameproof
baking dish*

If cool or warm, the meat is not yet done. When checking the meat, also check the potatoes to be sure they do not dry out. If so, add a little more stock.

When the pork is cooked, cut off the strings and set the meat on a carving board. Bring the gravy to the boil, adjust seasoning and pour into a serving bowl. At the table, carve the meat into generous slices. Serve the gravy separately, with the potatoes in their baking dish.

ROAST PORK LOIN WITH CELERIAC & BACON

Adding celeriac and bacon maintains the Italian influence of this roast while giving a lighter alternative to a hearty country dish.

In the recipe above, add 180 g / 6 oz of bacon and replace the potatoes with a medium head of celeriac. Cut the bacon across into 5 mm / ¼ in strips, what the French call *lardons*. Put them in a pan over medium heat. Prepare the onions as above and stir into the bacon. Wash the celeriac and wipe it dry. Cut it in half from stem to root. Lay each half cut side down on a board and cut it into 2 cm / ¾ in slices. Stack 2 or 3 slices at a time and cut these into 2 cm / ¾ in sticks. Bunch the sticks and cut them across into dice. When the onions are soft, add the diced celeriac and stir until well mixed. Then spread them flat.

Bake the vegetables in the oven with the pork as described.

RECAP

1 PREHEAT OVEN TO 200°C/400°F/GAS6 — ALLOW 5-10 MINUTES FOR THIS BEFORE YOU START.

2 PEEL GARLIC AND PUT IN PROCESSOR. STRIP SAGE AND THYME LEAVES FROM STEMS AND ADD TO GARLIC WITH TEASPOON OF SALT AND 2 TABLESPOONS OIL. ROUGHLY CRUSH PEPPERCORNS AND ADD. WORK TO PURÉE.

3 TRIM EXCESS FAT FROM PORK AND SPREAD INSIDE WITH TWO-THIRDS OF HERB MIXTURE. ROLL AND TIE PORK WITH STRING. PUT WITH REMAINING OIL IN DEEP FLAMEPROOF CASSEROLE AND SEASON. BROWN OVER QUITE HIGH HEAT.

4 MEANWHILE, PREPARE POTATOES: HEAT OIL IN SHALLOW FLAMEPROOF BAKING DISH. PEEL AND SLICE ONION, ADD TO DISH AND LEAVE TO SAUTÉ. WASH AND DRY POTATOES. THINLY SLICE INTO PROCESSOR, LETTING FALL INTO REMAINING GARLIC PURÉE.

5 ADD POTATOES, SALT AND PEPPER TO ONIONS. STIR THOROUGHLY AND SPREAD FLAT. POUR OVER STOCK, COVER WITH FOIL AND BAKE 45-60 MINUTES, UNTIL POTATOES ARE VERY TENDER AND STOCK IS ABSORBED.

6 MEANWHILE TURN PORK BROWNED SIDE UP AND POUR OVER MILK. COVER AND COOK IN OVEN WITH POTATOES 45-60 MINUTES UNTIL A SKEWER INSERTED IN CENTRE IS HOT TO TOUCH WHEN WITHDRAWN AFTER 30 SECONDS.

7 WHEN PORK IS COOKED, TRANSFER TO CARVING BOARD. BOIL GRAVY, ADJUST SEASONING AND POUR INTO SERVING BOWL. SERVE POTATOES SEPARATELY, FROM BAKING DISH.

BAKED HAM WITH APPLES & CREAM

TIME IN KITCHEN
8 minutes
BAKING *15-20 minutes*
(5-7 in the microwave)

serves 4

The Normans don't produce a great variety of ingredients, but those few are superb. We had a house on the Channel coast for several years and my memories of the shellfish, the milk-fed veal, the cream and the crisp apples are vivid. In this recipe the apples are used with cream — crème fraîche if possible — and Calvados apple brandy to make a rich sauce for baked ham. If you have Granny Smith apples, they will add a pleasant tartness to the sauce but, unlike Golden Delicious, they will fall apart if you try to fry them in rings. Potatoes should be served with the ham — Normandy is not rice or pasta territory.

Few meats vary more from country to country than ham. In the USA, I'd look for a steak of cooked country ham cut at least 1 cm / ⅜ in thick. In England, gammon is a good bet, less expensive than ham and just as juicy in a dish like this. In France the charcutier should cut the steak for you from a robust 'jambon d'York'. Wherever you are, avoid the lowly pre-sliced processed ham. If that's all that is available, choose another recipe.

1 or 2 ham steaks, cut 1 cm / ⅜ in thick (about 750 g / 1½ lb)
45 g / 1½ oz butter
1 onion
2 apples
30 g / 1 oz sugar
3-4 tablespoons Calvados or Cognac
250 ml / 8 fl oz crème fraîche or double cream
salt and freshly ground black pepper

Preheat the oven to 200°C/400°F/gas6 – allow 5-10 minutes for this before you start the recipe.

Melt half the butter in a medium frying pan over a low heat. Meanwhile, peel the onion, leaving a little of the root. Cut it in half from stem to root and set it cut side down on a cutting board. Thinly slice it, again cutting from stem to root. Stir the onion into the butter and leave to cook gently.

Meanwhile, quarter one of the apples and scoop out the core. Thinly slice the quarters, letting the slices fall into the pan of onions. Sprinkle with a tablespoon of the sugar, salt and pepper and sauté quite briskly for 1-2 minutes. The onion and apple should soften and start to brown, taking on a flavour of caramel from the sugar.

Meanwhile, melt the remaining butter in another frying pan. Core the remaining apple, using an apple corer or a vegetable peeler, forcing it down through the centre of the apple, then twisting to loosen the core. Do not peel the apple, but cut it into rings 1 cm / ⅜ in thick, discarding the ends. Add the apple rings to the butter, sprinkle with a little more sugar and turn them sugar side down so they caramelize. Sprinkle the top with the remaining sugar and leave them to sauté over a medium heat for 2-3 minutes.

Meanwhile, take the pan of onion and apple from the heat, pour over the Calvados or Cognac and light it with a match, standing back as Calvados can make a tall flame. If it does not light, replace the pan on the heat, heat gently and try again. La Varenne chefs call this '*cinéma*'. The flames are certainly dramatic, but I think they do help to caramelize ingredients in the pan. When the flames die, it's a sign that the alcohol has burned off and you can move on. Take a look at the apple rings and turn them over if they are brown. Leave them to brown on the other side.

Cut the ham into 4 serving portions and lay in a baking dish or microwave dish.

Add the cream to the onions and apples and bring to the boil, stirring to dissolve the sticky juices on the bottom of the pan. The apple will have softened enough to thicken the cream lightly. Add salt and pepper to taste (remember the ham is salty) and pour over the ham, coating it completely. Cover with foil or microwave film. Bake until hot and bubbling, 15-20 minutes in the oven or 5-7 minutes in the microwave on high.

When the apple rings are browned, take them from the heat. Cover and keep them in a warm place. Serve the ham in the baking dish, topping it with the apple rings, or arrange a piece of ham on 4 individual plates, spoon over the sauce and top with an apple ring.

BAKED HAM IN PAPRIKA SAUCE

In the recipe above, the saltiness of ham is complemented by sweet apples. Here the apples are replaced by paprika for a marriage of salt and peppery spice — this recipe merits the best Hungarian sweet paprika, if you can find it. A hearty pasta, such as shells or macaroni, is the best accompaniment.

In the recipe above, omit the apples and sugar. Replace the Calvados with vodka. Sauté the onion for 1-2 minutes, then stir in 2 tablespoons of paprika. Cook gently for 1 minute to toast the paprika lightly, stirring constantly. Flame with the vodka, add the cream and bring to a boil. Continue as directed, baking the ham in the paprika sauce and omitting the garnish of apple rings.

RECAP

1 PREHEAT OVEN TO 200°C/400°F/GAS6 — ALLOW 5-10 MINUTES FOR THIS BEFORE YOU START.

2 MELT HALF BUTTER IN FRYING PAN. PEEL AND SLICE ONION, ADD TO BUTTER AND COOK GENTLY.

3 CORE AND SLICE 1 APPLE, LETTING SLICES FALL INTO PAN OF ONION. STIR IN 1 TABLESPOON OF SUGAR, SEASON AND SAUTÉ 1-2 MINUTES.

4 MEANWHILE, MELT REMAINING BUTTER IN ANOTHER FRYING PAN. CORE REMAINING APPLE AND CUT INTO 1 CM / ³/₈ IN RINGS, DISCARDING ENDS. ADD TO BUTTER, SPRINKLE WITH A LITTLE MORE SUGAR AND TURN SUGAR SIDE DOWN. SPRINKLE WITH REMAINING SUGAR AND SAUTÉ 2-3 MINUTES.

5 MEANWHILE, TAKE PAN OF ONION AND APPLE FROM HEAT AND FLAME WITH CALVADOS. REPLACE PAN ON HEAT, ADD CREAM AND BRING TO BOIL, STIRRING TO DISSOLVE STICKY JUICES ON BOTTOM OF PAN. SEASON TO TASTE. CHECK APPLE RINGS, TURN IF BROWN AND LEAVE 2-3 MINUTES TO BROWN ON OTHER SIDE.

6 CUT HAM INTO 4 SERVING PORTIONS AND LAY IN A BAKING DISH OR MICROWAVE DISH. POUR OVER SAUCE, COVER WITH FOIL OR MICROWAVE FILM AND BAKE UNTIL HOT AND BUBBLING: 15-20 MINUTES IN OVEN OR 5-7 MINUTES IN MICROWAVE ON HIGH.

7 WHEN APPLE RINGS ARE BROWNED, TAKE FROM HEAT, COVER AND KEEP WARM.

8 SERVE HAM FROM BAKING DISH OR TRANSFER WITH SAUCE TO 4 PLATES AND TOP WITH APPLE RINGS.

FIFTEEN MINUTES TO TABLE

It's surprising what can be cooked in 15 minutes, given a bit of imagination and a compliant main ingredient, such as fish, minute steak or veal escalope. For a simple satisfying meal, pasta must come near the top of most people's list. Try Bow-ties with Wild Mushrooms & Nuts or Oriental-style Stir-fried Rice Noodles with Prawns. Fresh tagliatelle is available now in most supermarkets and is delicious with coriander and ginger or use it in place of spaghetti with pungent Sicilian flavourings.

Even when you've had no time to get to the shops, if you follow the advice in The Well-stocked Store-cupboard (page 8) you can fall back on eggs, pasta or a quickly simmered vegetable soup. It will pay time and again to keep on hand items such as olive oil, wine vinegar and grated cheese, not to mention wine, garlic, spring onions and a herb or two.

I hope you'll consider the following recipes as a starting point, making the substitutions I suggest or inventing your own. For instance, you can fill the Open-faced Peasant Omelette with almost anything you happen to have on hand, from cooked chicken or fish to vegetables and cheese. Both the Stir-fried Rice Noodles with Prawns and the Spiced Indonesian Stir-fry recipes are equally accommodating.

Team any of the recipes in this section with something from Speedy Salads, such as Wilted Frisée with Bacon Salad, Panzanella or Crazy Salad, all of which take less than 15 minutes. Add a quick idea from Fast Finishes, like Strawberry Burnt Cream, Orange Salad with Caramel or Marmalade Soufflé and you have a three-course menu ready in less than an hour. So light the oven, heat a pot of water and pour yourself a drink, even if it's only a glass of sparkling water ... and relax!

left FIFTEEN-MINUTE MINESTRONE *see page 48*

FIFTEEN-MINUTE MINESTRONE

TIME IN KITCHEN
15 minutes

serves 4

I know purists may shudder at the notion of putting together a version of minestrone in 15 minutes, but it's precisely the integrity of such a classic recipe that makes it a good point of departure. Admittedly, for speed we have to omit slow-cooking vegetables like carrot, cabbage and fennel. Leek must take the place of onion, with quickly cooked pasta — like bows — instead of macaroni. For once I'm resorting to cans — tomato and kidney beans — but I think you'll be surprised what a satisfying soup can be simmered in such a short time.

This recipe begs to be made in larger quantities, as slicing more vegetables scarcely increases work time. Serve the soup right away to capture the burst of vegetable flavours. With a loaf of Italian bread, Fifteen-minute Minestrone becomes a meal in itself.

1 bay leaf
1 leek
3 celery stalks
2 tablespoons olive oil
175 g / 6 oz slice of
  country ham
1 garlic clove
2 small courgettes
50 g / 1½ oz pasta bows
1 small can of plum
  tomatoes
  (250 g / 8 oz)
1 small can of white
  kidney beans
  (250 g / 8 oz)
salt and freshly ground
  black pepper
4 sprigs of flat-leaf
  parsley, to decorate
60 g / 2 oz grated
  Parmesan cheese, to
  serve

Bring 1 litre / 1⅔ pt of water to the boil with the bay leaf in a large covered soup pot.

Trim the root and tough green tops of the leek and slit it in half lengthwise. Slice it across as thinly as possible. Cut the celery across in the thinnest possible slices. Wash the leek and celery slices under running water in a colander.

These two last vegetables take longest to cook, so they are sautéed apart from the others: heat the oil in a frying pan, add the celery and leek with some pepper. Cover with foil and leave to cook gently.

Discard any fat from the ham, cut the ham in strips, then across into dice. Add it to the pan of vegetables. Crush the garlic with the flat of the knife to loosen the skin and discard it. Crush the clove with the flat of the knife and chop it with the blade. Add the garlic to the vegetables, replacing the foil.

Trim off the ends of the courgettes, quarter them lengthwise, then cut them across into 1 cm / ⅜ in slices. Drop into the pan of boiling water and add a little pepper — remember that the ham will add more salt. Stir in the pasta, and replace the cover.

Drain the tomatoes and add the juice to the soup. Coarsely chop the tomatoes and add them. Stir in the can of beans with their liquid.

By now the leeks and celery should be soft. Stir into the soup, together with the ham and garlic. Bring to the boil and simmer for 3-4 minutes to blend the flavours.

Discard the bay leaf and adjust the seasoning (salt may not be needed as the ham is salty). Spoon the soup into bowls and top with a sprig of parsley. Serve grated Parmesan cheese separately.

RECAP

1 BRING 1 LITRE / 1⅔ PT WATER TO BOIL WITH BAY LEAF IN LARGE COVERED SOUP POT.

2 SLICE LEEKS AND CELERY AND WASH. HEAT OIL IN FRYING PAN, ADD SLICED VEGETABLES WITH PEPPER AND COVER WITH FOIL. COOK GENTLY UNTIL SOFT.

3 MEANWHILE, DICE HAM AND ADD TO PAN. PEEL AND CHOP GARLIC AND ADD.

4 TRIM, QUARTER AND SLICE COURGETTES. ADD TO POT OF BOILING WATER WITH SOME PEPPER. STIR IN PASTA AND COVER PAN.

5 DRAIN TOMATOES AND ADD JUICE TO SOUP. COARSELY CHOP TOMATOES

AND ADD. STIR IN BEANS, THEN ADD VEGETABLES, HAM AND GARLIC.

6 COVER, BRING TO BOIL AND SIMMER 3-4 MINUTES.

7 ADJUST SEASONING, SPOON INTO BOWLS AND TOP WITH PARSLEY SPRIGS. SERVE GRATED PARMESAN SEPARATELY.

SALMON ESCALOPES WITH MUSTARD SAUCE

TIME IN KITCHEN
10 minutes

serves 4

I rarely use a non-stick frying pan — by definition, it doesn't brown food well since nothing sticks — but here a non-stick surface is essential for the rapid cooking of thin salmon escalopes using almost no fat. Then we whisk up a quick sauce in the pan with cream, mustard and tarragon — an unexpected but classic combination found in lobster Thermidor.

Be sure to have the line of bones along the centre of the salmon fillet removed at the fish counter, as taking them out yourself with a pair of tweezers will tax your patience.

You can even vary a recipe as simple as this by using a different mustard — perhaps one with seeds, or flavoured with orange. Monkfish instead of salmon is also a possibility.

1 large fillet of salmon with the skin, weighing about 625 g / 1¼ lb

1 medium carrot

knob of butter

250 ml / 8 fl oz double cream

small bunch of tarragon

2 teaspoons Dijon-style mustard, or more to taste

salt and freshly ground black pepper

Put a small pan of salted water on to heat, cover and bring to the boil — allow 5 minutes for this before you start the recipe.

To cut the carrot into julienne strips: trim the ends but don't bother to peel it. Cut a slice from one side so the carrot sits flat, then cut it lengthwise into the thinnest possible slices. Stack 3-4 slices at a time and cut into very thin strips. They will be of uneven length. Simmer in the boiling water for 4-5 minutes, until just tender.

Meanwhile, using a large chef's knife, cut the salmon escalopes. Work away from you towards the tail end of the fillet. Cut large diagonal slices about 1 cm / ⅜ in thick, leaving the skin behind. There should be at least 8 slices. Sprinkle with salt and pepper.

Heat the non-stick frying pan. Drain the carrot julienne and reserve it. Brush the hot pan with a little butter and add half the escalopes. Cook over a high heat for 30-60 seconds until lightly browned, turn and brown the other side for 30-60 seconds longer. If overdone, the escalopes will fall apart — they should remain slightly translucent in the centre. Transfer to a plate and keep warm while you cook the remaining escalopes.

Add the cream to the pan and bring to the boil. Meanwhile, strip the tarragon leaves from the stems and chop the leaves very coarsely so they are not bruised. Whisk the mustard into the sauce — it will emulsify and thicken the sauce slightly. Whisk in the chopped tarragon, carrot julienne and a little salt and pepper. Adjust the seasoning.

Arrange the escalopes on 4 warmed plates and spoon the sauce on top, leaving some of the pretty pink salmon showing.

RECAP

1 BRING SMALL COVERED PAN OF SALTED WATER TO BOIL — ALLOW **5** MINUTES FOR THIS BEFORE YOU START.

2 TRIM CARROT AND CUT INTO JULIENNE STRIPS. SIMMER IN WATER **4-5** MINUTES.

3 MEANWHILE, CUT SALMON FILLET INTO 1 CM / ⅜ IN ESCALOPES, DISCARDING SKIN. SEASON.

4 HEAT FRYING PAN. DRAIN AND RESERVE CARROT JULIENNE. BRUSH HOT PAN WITH BUTTER, ADD HALF ESCALOPES AND COOK OVER HIGH HEAT **30-60** SECONDS UNTIL BROWN. TURN AND BROWN ON OTHER SIDES, **30-60** SECONDS LONGER. REMOVE AND COOK THE REMAINING ESCALOPES IN SAME WAY.

5 ADD CREAM TO PAN AND BRING TO BOIL. MEANWHILE STRIP TARRAGON LEAVES FROM STEMS AND COARSELY CHOP. WHISK MUSTARD, TARRAGON, CARROT JULIENNE, SALT AND PEPPER INTO SAUCE AND ADJUST SEASONING.

6 ARRANGE ESCALOPES ON 4 WARMED PLATES AND SPOON OVER SAUCE.

BOW-TIES WITH WILD
MUSHROOMS & NUTS

TIME IN KITCHEN
13 minutes

serves 4

This recipe is an indulgence, for even a modest box of shiitake mushrooms comes expensive. To make them go further, you can substitute equal quantities of cultivated white mushrooms without losing much intensity of flavour. Even better, I find, is to add a few dried mushrooms, which can be surprisingly cheap — especially in Oriental stores. Dried shiitake are good, and Chinese black mushrooms even better. Best of all are dried morels — you may wince at the price, but just a few will perfume the whole dish.

To highlight the earthy flavour of the mushrooms I've added toasted hazelnuts. Try to find peeled hazelnuts, otherwise after roasting them you'll have to spend time rubbing them to remove the skin. The sauce is rich, so we need a shaped pasta which will absorb and hold it, such as bow-ties, shells, fusilli — even familiar macaroni. If you try noodles or spaghetti you'll find all the garnish falls to the bottom of the bowl.

**125 g / 4 oz peeled
hazelnuts**

**60 g / 2 oz dried
mushrooms, such as
shiitake**

**500 g / 1 lb dried bow-
tie pasta**

**250 g / ½ lb fresh wild
mushrooms, such as
shiitake or
chanterelles**

2 garlic cloves

45 g / 1½ oz butter

**125 ml / 4 fl oz white
wine**

**250 ml / 8 fl oz double
cream**

**salt and freshly ground
black pepper**

Preheat the oven to 200°C/400°F/gas6. Put a large pan of salted water on to heat, cover and bring to the boil. Allow 5-10 minutes for this before you start the recipe.

Spread the hazelnuts on a baking sheet and put them in the preheated oven to toast. They will take 8-10 minutes and you'll need to keep an eye on them towards the end of cooking. The best way is to use your nose — when you smell them, they're done.

Put the dried mushrooms in a small bowl and ladle over enough boiling water to cover them. Stir the pasta into the remaining boiling water, bring it back to the boil and simmer uncovered for 8-10 minutes. Stir the pasta once or twice during cooking and, if the pan tends to boil over, add a spoonful of oil to cut the foam.

Trim the stems of fresh mushrooms (shiitake stems are very tough and must be removed level with the caps) and brush away any soil. Wash them only if they are very sandy, soaking them briefly in cold water then lifting them out with your hands so grit is left behind. Cut them into large pieces.

With the flat of the knife, lightly crush the garlic cloves to loosen the skin and discard it. With the flat of the knife, smash the cloves, then chop them.

Melt the butter in a large frying pan. While it is heating, take time to stir the pasta and look at the hazelnuts, rolling them to turn them over. Add the mushrooms, garlic, salt and pepper to the frying pan and stir to mix. Leave them to sauté over a high heat while you prepare the dried mushrooms. Drain them, trim the stems and cut the caps into pieces. Stir them into the fresh mushrooms and add the wine. Continue simmering for 2-3 minutes, until most of the liquid has evaporated.

Meanwhile, check again on the pasta and hazelnuts. When the nuts are brown, remove them from the oven and spread them on a large sheet of plastic film. Roll the nuts in the film and pound them about 5 times with a rolling pin to crush them lightly, leaving some chunks. The pasta is done when a piece feels chewy but not hard to your bite — 'al dente'. When cooked, drain it and return it to the pan to keep warm.

Stir the cream into the mushrooms and bring the sauce to the boil. Taste and adjust the seasoning. Pour it over the pasta, add the hazelnuts and replace the pan over a medium heat. Toss the pasta for 30-60 seconds until it is very hot, then taste and adjust the seasoning again. You'll find that wooden spoons or forks are best for tossing, as they do not cut the pasta. Serve it in a large warm bowl or on individual plates.

RECAP

1 PREHEAT OVEN TO 200°C/400°F/GAS 6. BRING LARGE PAN OF SALTED WATER TO BOIL — ALLOW *5-10* MINUTES FOR THIS.

2 SPREAD NUTS ON BAKING SHEET AND BAKE *8-10* MINUTES UNTIL BROWNED.

3 LADLE BOILING WATER OVER DRIED MUSHROOMS AND LEAVE TO SOAK. SIMMER PASTA IN REMAINING BOILING WATER *8-10* MINUTES UNTIL 'AL DENTE'.

4 MEANWHILE, TRIM FRESH MUSHROOM STEMS, BRUSH CAPS AND CUT INTO LARGE PIECES. CHOP GARLIC.

5 MELT BUTTER IN LARGE FRYING PAN, SAUTÉ FRESH MUSHROOMS, GARLIC, SALT AND PEPPER OVER HIGH HEAT.

6 DRAIN DRIED MUSHROOMS, TRIM STEMS AND CUT CAPS INTO PIECES. STIR INTO FRESH MUSHROOMS, ADD WINE AND SIMMER *2-3* MINUTES UNTIL MOST HAS EVAPORATED.

7 WHEN THE NUTS ARE BROWN, REMOVE THEM. ROLL IN SHEET OF PLASTIC FILM AND LIGHTLY CRUSH WITH ROLLING PIN. WHEN PASTA IS COOKED, DRAIN AND RETURN TO PAN.

8 STIR CREAM INTO MUSHROOMS, BRING TO BOIL AND ADJUST SEASONING. ADD TO PASTA WITH NUTS, RETURN TO HEAT AND TOSS *30-60* SECONDS UNTIL VERY HOT. ADJUST SEASONING AND SERVE.

FIFTEEN-MINUTE
FIRE POT

TIME IN KITCHEN
15 minutes

serves 4

I hesitate to give this simplified recipe the classic title of Mongolian Firepot or Hot-pot, though this is the source of my idea. On a burner with a sturdy stand in the centre of the dining table goes a generous pot of boiling water flavoured with ginger and salt. Each guest receives a generous plate of slivers of raw beef, scallops, bean curd and vegetables for dipping into the hot-pot with chopsticks. As the meal progresses, the pot is more and more powerfully infused with flavourings. Finally, the few remaining ingredients are added to the pot, simmered with some noodles and the broth served as a steaming aromatic bowl of soup to round off the meal.

To keep the pot on the simmer, you'll need quite a strong flame — higher than the average spirit burner for fondue. If you have doubts about the heat, when the pot first comes to the table ask your guests to give priority to dipping beef and scallops. When the water cools, tip the remaining bean curd and vegetables into the pot, return it to the stove and reheat it, simmering it for 1 minute. Add the coriander and vermicelli, and simmer for 1 minute longer, then ladle this savoury soup into serving bowls and return it to the table.

To minimize work time on this recipe we're very dependent on the goodwill of your butcher in cutting the beef wafer-thin with his electric slicer. In these days of the fashion for 'carpaccio', which also depends on thinly sliced raw beef, many butchers are familiar with this request. If not, here's what to do: wrap the piece of fillet in foil and chill it in the freezer until half frozen, about 3 hours. Then cut it into the thinnest possible slices with a sharp knife, working diagonally across the grain.

**500 g / 1 lb raw beef
fillet, cut in very
thin slices**
125 g / 4 oz scallops
**125 g / 4 oz soft bean
curd**
**250 g / ½ lb washed
baby spinach or
1 large bunch of
watercress**
**1 small head of
bok-choy
(about 375 g / ¾ lb)**
4 spring onions
**small bunch of fresh
coriander**
**45 g / 1½ oz medium
rice noodles**

Put 2 litres / 3¼ pt of water in the pot with the salt, cover with a lid and bring to the boil. It should not take more than 10 minutes. Meanwhile, slice the ginger without peeling it and add to the pot. Be sure to cut across the grain to release more flavour. Turn the heat off once the water comes to a boil so that liquid does not evaporate while you prepare the other ingredients — if you keep the cover on, it will take no time to bring back to a boil when you are ready to sit down at the table.

Next, prepare the individual plates of ingredients. Set out 4 large plates and arrange the beef slices at one side, pleating them slightly. Pat the scallops dry on paper towel and discard the crescent-shaped membrane to one side of the main muscle. If the scallops are large, cut each one across into 2 discs; if small, leave them whole. Arrange overlapping on the plates. Cut the bean curd in large cubes and pile on the plates.

Discard any large stems from the spinach and pile the leaves on the plates. If using watercress, rinse in cold water, shake dry and twist off the stems. Pile the watercress leaves on the plates. Trim the bok-choy root, discard any wilted outer leaves. Cut it in half lengthwise, lay each half cut side down and cut the leaves across into 2.5 cm / 1 in slices. Pile them on the plates. Trim the spring onions, leaving some of the green stems, and add them to the plates. They are left whole to be eaten raw or dipped in the pot, whichever the diner prefers.

Chop the coriander and put it in a small bowl so that it can be added to the pot along with the rice noodles.

Make the sauce: put the tahini paste, soy sauce, the chilli paste or Tabasco and the vinegar in a bowl and stir until smooth. Stir in about 4 tablespoons of water. Taste the

for the pot:
1 tablespoon salt
walnut-sized piece of
 ginger

for the sauce:
125 g / 4 oz tahini paste
2 teaspoons dark soy
 sauce
2 teaspoons red chilli
 paste or a few drops
 Tabasco sauce
4 teaspoons rice or red
 wine vinegar

table burner
large shallow pot
4 pairs of chopsticks

sauce and adjust the proportions. It is intended as a condiment and may be soothing, piquant or hot, as you prefer. Put the sauce in 4 small dipping bowls.

Transfer the pot – which should now be boiling – to the table burner. Adjust the heat so the liquid simmers. Set plates of meat and vegetables at each place, with chopsticks and a bowl of sauce.

Invite each guest to dip meat, scallops, bean curd and vegetables into the pot at will, cooking them to taste and then dipping into the sauce. If the flame on your pot is not very strong, you should advise your guests to cook their meat and scallops first.

Towards the end of the meal, add the rice noodles and chopped coriander to the pot together with any uncooked ingredients which may remain and bring the soup back to the boil. You may need to take it back to the hob to bring it to a full boil. Simmer for 1 minute, until the noodles are just tender. This small break will come as a welcome pause for your guests between courses.

Ladle the soup into 4 serving bowls and pass to your guests to end the meal. Any leftover sauce can be stirred into the soup to add some spice. Even this simple version of Mongolian fire-pot is a feast.

RECAP

1 BRING 2 LITRES / 3¼ PT WATER TO BOIL IN COVERED POT WITH SALT AND SLICED GINGER.

2 ARRANGE BEEF SLICES AT SIDES OF 4 PLATES. PAT SCALLOPS DRY, DISCARD MEMBRANE AND ADD TO PLATES. CUT BEAN CURD IN LARGE CUBES AND ADD.

3 DISCARD STEMS FROM SPINACH. IF USING WATERCRESS, RINSE BUNCHES, SHAKE DRY AND TWIST OFF STEMS. TRIM BOK-CHOY, CUT IN 2.5 CM / 1 IN SLICES. TRIM SPRING ONIONS. ARRANGE VEGETABLES ON PLATES.

4 CHOP CORIANDER AND PUT IN SMALL BOWL.

5 MAKE SAUCE: STIR TOGETHER TAHINI, SOY SAUCE, CHILLI PASTE OR TABASCO AND VINEGAR WITH ABOUT 4 TABLESPOONS WATER; ADJUST PROPORTIONS TO TASTE. PUT IN 4 INDIVIDUAL BOWLS.

6 TRANSFER POT TO TABLE BURNER. SET PLATES OF MEAT AND VEGETABLES AT EACH PLACE, WITH CHOPSTICKS AND BOWL OF SAUCE.

7 TOWARDS END OF THE MEAL, ADD RICE NOODLES AND CORIANDER TO POT AND SIMMER 1 MINUTE UNTIL JUST TENDER. IF POT LOSES TOO MUCH HEAT DURING MEAL, ADD ALL REMAINING INGREDIENTS AND RETURN POT TO HOB TO FINISH COOKING.

STIR-FRIED RICE NOODLES WITH PRAWNS

TIME IN KITCHEN
10 minutes

serves 4

I was introduced to the wok after many years of using only French kitchen equipment and became an instant fan. The wide rounded surface makes it easy to cook a sizeable quantity of food, while the wok stirrer — its edge curved to match the pan — doubles as a scoop.

Due to the almost instantaneous transfer of heat through the thin metal of the wok, stir-frying is one of the quickest of techniques. Even so, to hit the 15-minute work time you'll need to reduce preparation by using peeled cooked prawns and prepared chilli. Best of all is Chinese red chilli paste, but dried chilli flakes will do — allow about ½ teaspoon.

For a less expensive dish, you can substitute fillets of white fish, cutting them in strips — they cook in about a minute, the same time it takes to heat the prawns. If rice noodles are not available, substitute fresh angel-hair pasta.

2 garlic cloves

walnut-sized piece of fresh ginger

5-7 spring onions

3 tablespoons soy sauce, or more to taste

1 teaspoon Chinese red chilli paste, or more to taste

375 g / ¾ lb thin rice noodles

4 tablespoons vegetable oil

375 g / ¾ lb small peeled cooked prawns

1 teaspoon Oriental sesame oil, or more to taste

food processor
wok and stirrer

Bring a medium-sized pan of salted water to the boil with the lid on — allow 5-10 minutes for this before you start the recipe.

To peel the garlic cloves, crush them slightly with the flat of the knife to loosen the skin, and discard it. I don't bother to peel the ginger but simply cut it into chunks. Now trim the roots and tough green ends of the spring onions and cut the green parts into 1 cm / ⅜ in slices — a diagonal cut produces more attractive-looking pieces.

Put the white parts of the spring onions in the food processor with the garlic and ginger. Pulse for 15-30 seconds until everything is chopped. Stir together the soy sauce and chilli paste in a small bowl. The water should be boiling by this time. Add the noodles, stir and simmer for 1-2 minutes, until they are tender but still chewy.

Meanwhile, begin the stir-frying: pour the vegetable oil around the sides of the wok and heat for about 10 seconds, just until it starts to smoke. Immediately add the garlic, ginger and spring onion mixture with the prawns and stir-fry, using a wok stirrer, for 45 seconds to 1 minute, until fragrant. Take the wok from the heat until the noodles are cooked. Drain them, add them to the wok and return it to the heat. Toss and stir with the stirrer and a spoon for 1-2 minutes, until the prawns and noodles are very hot. To make best use of the heated surface when you are stir-frying, spread the ingredients up the sides of the pan as you stir rather than letting them collect in the bottom.

Lastly, add the soy sauce and chilli paste and stir-fry for 20-30 seconds to blend the flavours. Add the spring onion tops and sprinkle with the sesame oil. Stir and taste, adding more soy, chilli paste and sesame oil if you wish.

Serve at once, while very hot and fragrant — the essence of Asia!

STIR-FRIED RICE NOODLES WITH BLACK MUSHROOMS

Black Chinese mushrooms make a spectacular contrast to the white of rice noodles in this vegetarian recipe. In the recipe above, replace the prawns with 15 g / ½ oz dried black Chinese mushrooms. When you begin preparation, cover the mushrooms generously with boiling water and leave them to soak. Chop the leaves of a small bunch of coriander.

When the flavouring vegetables have been chopped, drain the mushrooms and slice them. Follow the recipe as described, stir-frying the mushrooms in place of the prawns, and stirring in the chopped coriander at the end of cooking.

RECAP

1 Bring pan of salted water to boil — allow 5-10 minutes for this.

2 Peel garlic and cut ginger into chunks without peeling. Cut green parts of spring onions in diagonal slices. Chop garlic, ginger and white parts of spring onions in a food processor. Stir together chilli paste and soy sauce.

3 When water is boiling, add noodles and simmer 1-2 minutes, until tender but still chewy. Meanwhile, pour vegetable oil around sides of wok and heat for 10 seconds. Add garlic, ginger and spring onion mixture with prawns and stir-fry about 45-60 seconds. Add drained noodles, tossing and stirring until very hot.

4 Add soy sauce and chilli paste and stir-fry 20-30 seconds more to blend flavours. Sprinkle with sesame oil and mix in spring onion greens. Serve at once.

OPEN-FACED OMELETTE
OF SMOKED HADDOCK

TIME IN KITCHEN
10 minutes

serves 4

I never understand why open-faced omelettes are not more popular as from the technical viewpoint they are even easier than the more common rolled or flat omelette. This recipe is a good example: the eggs are mixed with the filling, in this case flaked smoked haddock, and cooked in a large pan. They are then sprinkled with grated cheese and browned under the grill — no tricky folding or flipping needed.

All sorts of flavourings blend well with the generous layer of egg — smoked salmon or mackerel can take the place of haddock. Below I also suggest a 'paysanne' variation of bacon, croûtons and sorrel. An open-faced omelette is a great home for leftovers of cooked fish and vegetables. With the addition of a green salad and a crusty baguette, there's dinner on the table.

375 g / ¾ lb smoked haddock fillets
250 ml / 8 fl oz milk
8 eggs
60 g / 2 oz grated Parmesan cheese
30 g / 1 oz butter
125 ml / 4 fl oz double cream
salt and freshly ground black pepper

30 cm / 12 in omelette or frying pan

Preheat the grill — allow 5 minutes for this before you start the recipe.

Lay the haddock skin side up in a saucepan with the milk. Cover and simmer for 2-3 minutes until the fish flakes easily. Milk is often used for cooking smoked fish as it extracts salt and mellows the flavour of the fish.

While the fish is cooking, break the eggs into a bowl, add pepper and whisk for about 30 seconds, until frothy and well mixed. The fish and cheese will contribute salt.

Drain the fish and spread it, again skin side up, on a cold plate. There's no time to leave it to cool, so peel off the skin with two forks, flake the flesh and pick out any bones with your fingers. Stir the fish and half of the grated cheese into the eggs.

Add the butter to an omelette or frying pan and heat until it stops sputtering and just starts to brown. The browned butter adds flavour, but more importantly the very hot butter ensures that the eggs start cooking quickly and are less likely to stick in the pan. Have a fork ready for stirring.

Add the egg mixture to the browned butter and stir very briskly with the flat of the fork for 20-30 seconds, until the eggs start to cook and thicken.

Holding the fork upright, pull the cooked edges of egg from the sides of the pan to the centre, tipping the pan so the uncooked eggs run to the sides. Continue until the eggs are lightly set on the bottom but still soft on top. Leave the omelette for about 30 seconds without stirring to let the bottom brown.

Take the pan from the heat, pour the cream over the eggs and sprinkle them with the remaining grated cheese. Put the omelette under the grill about 5 cm / 2 in from the heat for about 2 minutes until brown. Ideally, I like the omelette to be lightly cooked with the eggs fairly soft. If you prefer better done, grill it farther from the heat for a slightly longer time. Serve the omelette at once, cut into wedges.

OPEN-FACED PEASANT OMELETTE

This recipe is a classic, an adaptation from Escoffier. I've substituted bread cubes for potato, as they cook more quickly, and added a topping of cheese. In the above recipe, omit the haddock, cream and milk. Substitute Gruyère for the Parmesan.

Dice 125 g / ¼ lb thickly sliced smoked bacon. Melt 1 tablespoon of the butter in a large frying pan and cook bacon over a quite high heat until it starts to brown.

Meanwhile, discard the crusts from 3 slices of white bread and cut the bread into dice. Add the bread to the bacon and cook, stirring constantly, for 30-60 seconds, until the bread is browned. Take the pan from the heat.

Loosely roll the leaves of small bunch of sorrel or rocket, or a handful of spinach leaves. Cut them across into shreds and discard the stems. Stir the shreds into the eggs with the bacon mixture.

Cook the omelette as described, sprinkling all of the cheese on top of the omelette instead of adding some to the eggs.

RECAP

1 Preheat grill — allow 5 minutes for this before you start.

2 Simmer haddock skin side up in milk 2-3 minutes, until it flakes. Drain and flake, discarding skin and bones.

3 While fish cooks, whisk eggs with pepper but no salt. Stir fish and half cheese into eggs.

4 Melt butter in omelette or frying pan and heat until just starting to brown. Add eggs and cook, stirring with a fork, until eggs are lightly set on bottom. Leave to brown base for 30 seconds.

5 Take pan from heat, pour cream over eggs and sprinkle with remaining cheese. Grill omelette close to heat about 2 minutes until brown. Serve at once, cut in wedges.

VEAL PICCATINE WITH MUSHROOMS & MARSALA

TIME IN KITCHEN
11 minutes

serves 4

'Piccatine' is the Venetian name for tiny veal escalopes, thinly cut and served 3 to 4 per person. You can cut them from larger escalopes as I suggest here, or your butcher might have some inexpensive trimmings on offer. Always buy top-quality — escalope should be moist, lightly pink and fine-textured, showing it has been cut from the topside or silverside. The best escalope may seem expensive, but a little goes a long way. Imitations cut from other parts of the animal are tough and tasteless.

I often make the same recipe with pork tenderloin, which is economical and easy to find. Trim any fat from the meat and cut it thinly on the diagonal — you'll have slices which are just the right size for piccatine. As a last quick thought, how about boneless chicken breasts? They are equally easy to slice diagonally and they cook well thus, with none of the dryness which afflicts a whole breast.

Marsala is traditional for this Italian dish, but a medium sherry can be substituted. I hope you've time to boil some rice to soak up the luscious sauce. As for an accompanying wine, red or white will do equally well — to be authentic, go Italian with a Pinot Grigio or Chianti Classico for example.

4 veal escalopes
  (about 500 g / 1 lb)
125 g / 4 oz mushrooms
60 g / 2 oz flour
1 teaspoon salt, or
  more to taste
½ teaspoon pepper, or
  more to taste
60 g / 2 oz butter
125 ml / 4 fl oz dry
  Marsala
125 ml / 4 fl oz double
  cream

Trim the stems of the mushrooms level with the caps. Wipe the caps with a damp cloth, but there is no need to wash them unless they are sandy. If so, drop them into a large bowl of cold water and stir so the sand falls to the bottom, then lift out with your hands. Set them stem side down on a board, thinly slice and put in a bowl.

Cover the chopping board with a sheet of plastic film. Set the escalopes flat on this and cover with another sheet. Wet the bottom of a small, heavy saucepan and pound the escalopes to flatten them. Don't overdo this; we want them to be of even thickness without breaking up the meat fibres. Cut them into 3 or 4 pieces.

Put the flour on a plate with the salt and pepper and mix with your fingers. Take the plate and piccatine to the stove, together with a spare plate to warm.

Heat half the butter in a large frying pan over quite a high heat. Dip some of the piccatine in the flour, patting with your hands so they are well coated on both sides. As soon as the butter stops sputtering, showing the whey has evaporated, fill the pan with piccatine. They should not touch each other and must fry quickly, so they brown without allowing their juices to be drawn out. Leave them to brown for 30-60 seconds while you finish coating the remaining pieces. Turn the piccatine and brown the other sides, 30-60 seconds longer. Transfer them to the warmed plate. Fry the remaining piccatine in 2 or 3 batches, adding a little more butter if the pan gets dry. Transfer them all to the plate.

Melt the remaining butter in the pan and add the mushrooms with some salt and pepper. Cook, stirring, for about 2 minutes until they are tender. They will render liquid which you should allow to reduce until they are almost dry.

Add the Marsala and simmer, stirring to dissolve the sticky juices on the bottom of the pan, until reduced by about half. Stir in the cream and bring it to the boil — thanks to the flour which coated the piccatine, it will thicken slightly and form a rich sauce.

Replace the piccatine in the sauce and heat gently for about 1 minute, but not longer or they will toughen and lose their juices. Adjust the seasoning of the sauce. Transfer the piccatine to 4 warmed plates and spoon the mushrooms and sauce on top.

RECAP

1 TRIM MUSHROOM STEMS, WIPE CAPS AND THINLY SLICE. POUND ESCALOPES BETWEEN TWO SHEETS OF PLASTIC FILM TO FLATTEN SLIGHTLY AND CUT INTO 3 OR 4 PIECES. MIX FLOUR ON A PLATE WITH SALT AND PEPPER.

2 HEAT HALF BUTTER IN LARGE FRYING PAN, MEANWHILE COATING SOME PICCATINE WITH FLOUR. ADD TO PAN AND FRY BRISKLY 30-60 SECONDS UNTIL BROWNED. TURN AND BROWN OTHER SIDES. IN MEANTIME, COAT REMAINING PICCATINE WITH FLOUR. TRANSFER BROWNED PICCATINE TO PLATE AND FRY REMAINDER, ADDING MORE BUTTER IF PAN SEEMS DRY. TRANSFER ALL MEAT TO PLATE.

3 MELT REMAINING BUTTER IN PAN AND ADD MUSH-ROOMS WITH SEASONING. COOK OVER HIGH HEAT FOR ABOUT 2 MINUTES, STIRRING UNTIL ALMOST ALL THEIR LIQUID EVAPORATES.

4 ADD MARSALA AND SIMMER, STIRRING, UNTIL PAN JUICES REDUCED BY HALF. STIR IN CREAM AND BRING TO BOIL SO IT THICKENS SLIGHTLY TO FORM SAUCE.

5 REPLACE PICCATINE TO HEAT GENTLY FOR ABOUT I MINUTE AND ADJUST SAUCE SEASONING.

TUNA STEAK MARCHAND DE VIN

TIME IN KITCHEN
10 minutes

serves 4

In France, the culinary term 'marchand de vin' denotes the standard way of pan-frying a juicy beef entrecôte with a finishing touch of red wine, shallots and herbs. Since tuna is virtually the 'steak' of the 'nineties, however, why not give it the same treatment. Delicious!

Swordfish is an alternative to the tuna, and your favourite herb can take the place of tarragon — chives, chervil and dill are particularly good. The only catch is that you must not use a cast-iron or aluminium frying pan or you will end up with a grey metallic sauce.

A white wine is traditional with fish, but this kind of dish can take red equally well — if not better. A red Loire wine, slightly chilled, would be a contemporary choice. If you have time, Chicory Salad with Goats' Cheese Toasts (see page 87) is a wonderful accompaniment.

4 tuna steaks
(about 625 g / 1¼ lb
in total)
60 g / 2 oz cold
unsalted butter
2 shallots
small bunch of
tarragon
2-3 parsley sprigs
250 ml / 8 fl oz red
wine
salt and freshly ground
black pepper

Cut the butter into cubes. Melt one-quarter in a heavy frying pan and heat until foaming. Meanwhile, sprinkle the tuna steaks on each side with salt and pepper. Add to the pan and sauté over quite a high heat for about 2 minutes.

Meanwhile, peel the shallots, leaving on a little of the root. If they do not have a flat side, cut a thin slice from one side. Set them flat side down and slice very thinly. If you've got time, slice another shallot too, the more the better.

Turn the steaks and brown the other side, 1-2 minutes. Strip the herbs from the stems. Return to check the tuna: test the centre of a steak with a knife — if you want it really rare, the outside should be seared but the centre still soft and translucent. Personally I prefer fish better done, with only a thin translucent line left in the centre.

Transfer the tuna to a warmed plate, cover and keep it warm. Come back to your herbs and chop all the leaves together — when mixed with parsley, the tarragon leaves are less likely to bruise and be bitter.

To make the sauce: add the shallots to the frying pan and sauté them for about 1 minute if you like them crisp, or about 2 minutes if you prefer them soft. Add the red wine and boil rapidly until reduced by about half.

Take the pan from the heat, add the remaining cubes of cold butter all at once and whisk vigorously until the butter softens and thickens the sauce slightly. Stir in the chopped herbs and adjust the seasoning.

Set the tuna steaks on 4 warmed plates, spoon over the sauce and serve at once.

RECAP

1 CUT BUTTER INTO CUBES AND HEAT ONE-QUARTER IN HEAVY FRYING PAN UNTIL FOAMING.

2 SEASON TUNA STEAKS, ADD TO PAN AND SAUTÉ OVER QUITE HIGH HEAT ABOUT 2 MINUTES.

3 MEANWHILE, PEEL AND THINLY SLICE SHALLOTS. TURN STEAKS AND BROWN OTHER SIDES, ABOUT 1-2

MINUTES. STRIP HERBS FROM STEMS.

4 TEST STEAKS IN CENTRE WITH SMALL KNIFE, COOKING TO RARE OR MEDIUM TO TASTE. TRANSFER TO WARM PLATE, COVER AND KEEP WARM. CHOP HERBS.

5 ADD SHALLOTS TO PAN AND SAUTÉ, STIRRING, 1-2 MINUTES. ADD WINE AND

BOIL RAPIDLY UNTIL REDUCED BY ABOUT HALF.

6 OFF HEAT, WHISK IN REMAINING BUTTER UNTIL IT SOFTENS AND THICKENS SAUCE SLIGHTLY. STIR IN CHOPPED HERBS AND TASTE FOR SEASONING.

7 TRANSFER STEAKS TO 4 WARMED PLATES AND SPOON OVER SAUCE.

SPICED INDONESIAN STIR-FRY

TIME IN KITCHEN
12 minutes

serves 4

I love all-purpose recipes which adapt easily to different ingredients. This is certainly one of them, since chicken, pork and beef marry well with the same zesty spice mix. Be sure to choose a tender cut that needs little trimming — for example, chicken breast, pork loin or fillet steak. The recipe includes a quick salad of crispy cucumber. Boiled rice, with perhaps some roasted peanuts for sprinkling, would be the traditional accompaniment.

750 g / 1½ lb boneless chicken breast, or fillet steaks, cut 2 cm / ¾ in thick, or boned pork loin

2 garlic cloves

½ teaspoon crushed dried red chilli pepper

2 teaspoons ground coriander

2 teaspoons ground ginger

3 tablespoons dark soy sauce

3 tablespoons rice vinegar

2 tablespoons groundnut or vegetable oil

for the cucumber salad:
1 large cucumber
small bunch of fresh coriander
250 ml / 8 fl oz plain yogurt
salt and freshly ground black pepper

wok and stirrer

First make the cucumber salad: peel the cucumber with a vegetable peeler, cut it lengthwise in half and scoop out the seeds with a teaspoon or the end of your vegetable peeler. Set each half on a chopping board and cut it into the thinnest possible slices.

Pull the coriander leaves from the stems, reserving 4 sprigs for garnish, and chop them coarsely with a large knife. Mix the cucumber in a bowl with the yogurt, chopped coriander, salt and pepper to taste and set aside.

Make the spice mix: lightly crush the garlic cloves with the flat of the knife to loosen the skin and discard. Crush the cloves with the flat of the knife and finely chop them with the knife blade. Put them in a bowl with the chilli, ground coriander, ginger, soy sauce and vinegar and stir to mix. Set aside.

If using chicken breasts, discard any skin. Cut the breast meat lengthwise into 2 or 3 strips, then cut these across into 2.5 cm / 1 in cubes. If using beef, trim any fat or sinew from the edge of the meat. Cut the steaks into 2 cm / ¾ in cubes. If using pork, trim any fat and cut the meat into 2.5 cm / 1 in slices, then into 2.5 cm / 1 in cubes. Trim any sinew from the cubes. The pieces will be uneven in shape, but try to keep them more or less the same size so they then cook evenly.

Heat the wok over a very high heat for 15 seconds, then drizzle the oil around the sides and heat until almost smoking. Add the cubes of chicken or meat and cook for about 2 minutes over a high heat, stirring constantly, until lightly browned.

Add the spice mix and stir-fry for 30-60 seconds longer depending on the meat: chicken and pork should be well done, and beef should be rare in the centre.

Pile the cucumber salad at the side of 4 individual plates, add the stir-fry and top each serving with a coriander sprig. Any accompaniments can be passed separately.

THAI STIR-FRY WITH WATERCRESS SALAD

Just a small change in flavouring evokes the fresh and vibrant flavours of Thailand. Watercress adds a crisp texture like that of the cucumber in the main recipe, with dark sesame oil to meld the flavours.

In the recipe above, replace the ground coriander and ginger with 2 stalks of lemon grass. Trim off the tough outer leaves and cut the stalks across into 5 mm / ¼ in slices. Add to the spice mix and finish the stir-fry as described above.

For the salad: whisk together 3 tablespoons of vegetable oil, 1 tablespoon of rice vinegar, 1 teaspoon of dark (Oriental) sesame oil, salt and freshly ground black pepper. Rinse and dry a medium bunch of watercress. Twist off the stalks. Mix the watercress leaves in a bowl with the dressing and 1 tablespoon of sesame seeds.

Serve the stir-fry with the salad at the side, or underneath it if you would like the watercress to wilt slightly.

RECAP

1 *Make cucumber salad: peel cucumber, slice lengthwise and scoop out seeds. Thinly slice and put in bowl. Chop coriander leaves, reserving 4 sprigs for garnish. Add chopped coriander to cucumbers with yogurt, salt and pepper. Mix well, taste and set aside.*

2 *Make spice mix: peel and chop garlic. Stir in a bowl with chilli,* ground coriander, ginger, soy sauce and vinegar. Set aside.

3 *If using chicken breasts, discard any skin and cut into 2.5 cm / 1 in cubes. For beef or pork, trim off any fat or sinew and cut into cubes.*

4 *To stir-fry: heat oil in wok until almost smoking. Add chicken or meat and stir-fry about 2 minutes until lightly browned.*

5 *Add spice mix and continue stir-frying 30-60 seconds, depending whether the meat should be rare or well done.*

6 *Pile cucumber salad at sides of 4 individual plates, add stir-fry, and top each serving with coriander sprig. Serve any accompaniments separately.*

PIQUANT STEAK WITH TOMATO

TIME IN KITCHEN
9 minutes

serves 4

8 minute steaks
(about 750 g / 1½ lb),
pounded flat
2 spring onions
3-4 parsley sprigs
1 large tomato
1 tablespoon oil
15 g / ½ oz butter
3 tablespoons Cognac
1 tablespoon
Worcestershire sauce
250 ml / 8 fl oz beef or
veal stock
salt and freshly ground
black pepper

Also known as 'Steak Diane', this recipe was created at the Dorchester in London. It is designed to be cooked in a chafing dish in the dining room, hence the flaming with Cognac. The flavour of the steak is less important than its tenderness, so you'll do best with minute steaks, cut from the thin tail end of the fillet. Two per person are enough, usually working out less expensive than a single fillet steak. Get the butcher to pound them flat. Boil some fresh pasta as an accompaniment.

Put a small deep pan of water on to heat, cover and bring to the boil — allow 5-10 minutes for this before you start the recipe.

Trim the spring onions and cut them in very thin diagonal slices — a diagonal cut always looks more attractive. Strip the parsley leaves from the stems and chop them.

Scoop out the core of the tomato with the point of a knife. Drop it into the boiling water and count slowly to 10. The skin should be peeling back from the cut around the core. If not, wait for another count of 5, then drain the tomato and hold it under cold running water. The skin will strip off easily. Cut the tomato across in half and squeeze each half so the seeds pop out. Set the halves cut side down on a board and slice. Turn the slices through 90 degrees and slice again into dice. Coarsely chop the dice. These actions, you'll be glad to know, take less time than reading about them.

Heat the oil and butter in the frying pan until the butter is foaming. Sprinkle the steaks with salt and pepper. Add half to the frying pan and fry over a high heat for 30-60 seconds until browned. Turn and brown the other sides for 30-60 seconds. Poke to ensure that they are still rare in the centre. Transfer to a warmed plate and keep warm while you brown the rest. Remove these too, then pour out any excess fat. With the pan off the heat, add the Cognac and light it with a match, standing back from the flames. Return the pan to the heat and keep cooking until the flames die.

Add the spring onions to the pan and cook for 30 seconds, until slightly soft. Stir in the tomato, Worcestershire sauce, stock, salt and pepper and bring to the boil. Replace the steaks, baste them with sauce and leave to heat for 1 minute.

Arrange steaks on 4 warmed plates. Stir parsley into sauce, adjust seasoning and simmer briefly to thicken if necessary. Spoon it over steaks and serve at once.

RECAP

1 BRING SMALL DEEP PAN OF WATER TO BOIL — ALLOW 5-10 MINUTES FOR THIS.

2 TRIM ONIONS AND CUT IN VERY THIN DIAGONAL SLICES. STRIP PARSLEY LEAVES FROM STEMS AND CHOP. CORE TOMATO, PEEL, SEED AND CHOP IT, USING BOILING WATER TO LOOSEN SKIN.

3 HEAT OIL AND BUTTER IN FRYING PAN. SEASON STEAKS.

ADD HALF TO PAN AND FRY OVER HIGH HEAT 30-60 SECONDS UNTIL BROWNED. TURN AND BROWN OTHER SIDES — THEY SHOULD STILL BE RARE IN CENTRE. TRANSFER TO WARMED PLATE AND COOK REMAINDER.

4 TAKE PAN FROM HEAT, POUR OFF EXCESS FAT, ADD COGNAC AND FLAME.

5 REPLACE ON HEAT, ADD

SPRING ONIONS AND SAUTÉ 30 SECONDS UNTIL WILTED. STIR IN TOMATO, WORCESTERSHIRE SAUCE, STOCK, SALT AND PEPPER. BRING TO BOIL. REPLACE STEAKS, BASTE WITH SAUCE AND HEAT 1 MINUTE.

6 ARRANGE STEAKS ON WARMED PLATES, STIR PARSLEY INTO SAUCE, ADJUST SEASONING AND SPOON OVER STEAKS.

See page 1

KEDGEREE

TIME IN KITCHEN
14 minutes

serves 4

Kedgeree is a striking golden-yellow mix of rice and smoked fish, spiced with curry and green with fresh herbs. For years it was my party piece, prepared ahead in large quantities for a leisurely Sunday brunch. I was very proud of it, until I went to India and tasted the real thing — a dark potent blend of aromatic spice, smoked fish pungent enough to survive the heat and cheap unpolished rice. It's only a memory, impossible to reproduce; but I think you'll enjoy this milder colonial version all the same. In Britain, the traditional fish to use is smoked haddock, but kippers and salmon are acceptable alternatives.

300 g / 10 oz long-grain white rice

500 ml / 16 fl oz milk

750 g / 1½ lb smoked haddock fillets

1 onion

45 g / 1½ oz butter

small bunch of fresh coriander or parsley

1 tablespoon curry powder

125 ml / 4 fl oz double cream

salt and freshly ground black pepper

pinch of cayenne (optional)

Put a large pan of salted water to heat, cover and bring to the boil. Allow 5-10 minutes for this before you start. When boiling, stir in the rice and leave to simmer for 10-12 minutes. To prevent it sticking, stir it once or twice again during cooking.

Heat the milk in a pan over medium heat. Cut the fish into 2 or 3 pieces. Put skin side up in the pan. Bring to the boil and simmer 2-3 minutes, until it flakes easily.

Now cook the onion: melt one-third of the butter in the frying pan over a low heat. Peel the onion and cut it in half through the root. Set the halves on a board and thinly slice. Add to the butter and leave to sauté for 1-2 minutes over a medium heat.

Test the fish and take it from the heat when cooked. Drain and transfer it to a plate to cool slightly. You'll find you can pull off the skin in one piece. Then flake the flesh, picking it over with a fork and discarding the bones. Take a moment to stir the rice.

Pull the coriander or parsley from the stems and chop the leaves. Test the rice by lifting out a few grains on a fork and tasting them. They should be firm and slightly chewy, but with no crunch to the centre. When cooked, drain in a colander and rinse very thoroughly with hot water. Rinse out the pan, add the remaining butter and heat until melted. Put the rice back and leave to warm over a very low heat.

Stir the curry powder into the onion and sauté for about 1 minute. Stir the fish and the cream into the onion and heat for about 1 minute until very hot. Add the fish mixture to the rice with the herbs and toss over a high heat until fragrant and very hot.

Taste the kedgeree and adjust the seasoning, adding salt, pepper and a pinch of cayenne if you like it hot. Serve the kedgeree in a serving bowl or on individual plates.

RECAP

1 BRING LARGE PAN OF SALTED WATER TO BOIL, ALLOW *5-10* MINUTES.

2 ADD RICE, STIR AND SIMMER *10-12* MINUTES.

3 HEAT MILK IN PAN. CUT FISH IN *2-3* PIECES AND ADD SKIN UP. SIMMER *2-3* MINUTES UNTIL IT FLAKES.

4 MELT ONE-THIRD OF BUTTER IN FRYING PAN. SLICE ONION, ADD AND SAUTÉ *1-2* MINUTES.

5 DRAIN FISH AND TRANSFER TO A PLATE. FLAKE WITH FINGERS, DISCARDING SKIN AND BONES. STIR RICE.

6 PULL HERB LEAVES FROM STEMS AND CHOP. TEST RICE BY TASTING FEW GRAINS — THEY SHOULD BE FIRM BUT NOT CRUNCHY. DRAIN IN COLANDER AND RINSE THOROUGHLY WITH HOT WATER. MELT REMAINING BUTTER IN PAN,

ADD RICE AND WARM OVER VERY LOW HEAT.

7 STIR CURRY POWDER INTO ONION AND COOK ABOUT *1* MINUTE. STIR IN FLAKED FISH AND CREAM AND HEAT UNTIL VERY HOT.

8 ADD FISH AND HERBS TO RICE AND TOSS OVER HIGH HEAT UNTIL FRAGRANT. ADJUST SEASONING, ADDING PINCH OF CAYENNE IF YOU LIKE.

EMMA'S SPAGHETTI WITH SAGE

TIME IN KITCHEN
11 minutes

serves 4

Our daughter Emma spent one summer on the island of Elba, cooking for the household of an economics professor who liked to put his classroom precepts into practice. The food budget was very small, the appetites of his research students hearty. This recipe using local olive oil and herbs from the garden was understandably a staple — Emma played half a dozen variations using basil, oregano or flat-leaf parsley instead of the sage. Sometimes she added chopped tomato, garlic or shallot to the herb leaves. By heating the oil before pouring it over the herb leaves you toast them just enough to develop their aroma without scorching. You might start the meal with a typically Italian salad like Panzanella (see page 74).

500 g / 1 lb spaghetti
2 large bunches of sage
125 ml / 4 fl oz olive oil
salt and freshly ground
black pepper
grated Parmesan
cheese, for serving

Put a large covered pan of salted water on to heat and bring it to the boil, allowing 5-10 minutes for this before you start the recipe.

When the water is boiling, add the spaghetti, holding the strands in your fist and letting them curl down into the bottom of the pan as they soften. When they are completely immersed, stir to separate the strands. Bring the water to a rolling boil, turn down the heat and leave the spaghetti to simmer, stirring once or twice. If it shows signs of boiling over, add a tablespoon of oil to cut the foam. Most spaghetti takes 8-10 minutes to cook. You can pinch it with your thumbnail, but the best test is to taste a strand; it should be firm and chewy ('al dente'), but not dry in the centre.

Meanwhile, pull the sage leaves from the stems. Loosely roll the leaves and coarsely shred them so they are not bruised. Put them in a large serving bowl. Heat the oil gently in a small pan. When the spaghetti is cooked, drain it in a colander.

When the oil is aromatic and almost starting to smoke. Pour it over the sage leaves – they should sizzle slightly. Add the drained spaghetti and mix vigorously with two wooden forks or spoons – for once the word 'toss' is appropriate. Season with salt and lots of ground black pepper. Serve at once, with a bowl of grated Parmesan cheese.

TAGLIATELLE WITH PARSLEY & PINE NUTS

If you use fresh tagliatelle, it cooks very quickly so prepare the other ingredients first.

Substitute flat-leaf parsley for the sage. Coarsely chop and put in serving bowl. Heat a tablespoon of the oil in a small frying pan and sauté 60 g / 2 oz pine nuts for 1-2 minutes until brown. Add to the parsley. Boil the tagliatelle, heat the oil and finish the recipe as described. Just before serving, sprinkle on a tablespoon of balsamic vinegar.

RECAP

1 BRING LARGE COVERED PAN OF SALTED WATER TO A BOIL, ALLOWING 5-10 MINUTES FOR THIS.

2 ADD SPAGHETTI, STIR AND SIMMER 8-10 MINUTES UNTIL JUST COOKED 'AL DENTE'. STIR FROM TIME TO TIME SO SPAGHETTI STRANDS DO NOT STICK.

3 PULL SAGE LEAVES FROM STEMS AND COARSELY SHRED LEAVES. PUT IN LARGE SERVING BOWL. HEAT OIL GENTLY IN A SMALL PAN.

4 WHEN SPAGHETTI IS COOKED, DRAIN IN COLANDER.

5 WHEN OIL IS ALMOST SMOKING, POUR OVER SAGE. ADD SPAGHETTI AND TOSS WELL. SPRINKLE WITH SALT AND PEPPER.

SICILIAN SPAGHETTI

TIME IN KITCHEN
9 minutes

serves 4

500 g / 1 lb spaghetti
3 garlic cloves
75 g / 2½ oz pitted
  oil-cured olives
60 g / 2 oz sun-dried
  tomatoes in oil
45 g / 1½ oz capers
½ teaspoon dried red
  pepper flakes, or
  more to taste
4 tablespoons olive oil
small bunch of flat-leaf
  parsley
salt and freshly ground
  black pepper

food processor

It's no accident that a young woman friend of Emma's contributed this recipe to the book — theirs is the pasta generation. I do particularly like this pungent sauce, reminiscent of the famous 'spaghetti alla puttanesca' or 'strumpets' spaghetti' — supposedly as strongly perfumed as Italian ladies of the night. Here the usual fresh tomatoes and anchovies are replaced by more subtle sun-dried tomatoes, and the ingredients are puréed to form a light sauce which coats the spaghetti. The sauce asks to be made in large quantities as it keeps well in a covered jar, at least a week in the refrigerator.

Put a large pan of salted water on to heat, cover and bring it to the boil. Allow 5-10 minutes for this before you start the recipe.

When the water is boiling, add the spaghetti, letting it curl down into the bottom of the pan as it softens. Stir it well so as to separate the strands, and leave to simmer 8-10 minutes. Stir the spaghetti several times during cooking so it does not stick and, if it shows signs of boiling over, add a tablespoon of oil to cut the foam. It is done when a strand of spaghetti is tender but still firm to the bite — 'al dente'.

Meanwhile, peel the garlic cloves, crushing them lightly with the flat of the knife to loosen the skin. Put the cloves in the processor with about three-quarters of the olives and sun-dried tomatoes, reserving a quarter of each for sprinkling on the cooked pasta. Drain the capers and set aside a quarter of them too, adding the rest to the processor.

Add the dried pepper flakes to the processor. Add the olive oil, reserving 1 tablespoon. Work the mixture to a smooth emulsified purée. What we've made is a hot version of Provençal tapenade, with dried tomatoes taking the place of anchovies.

While waiting for the spaghetti to cook, shred the reserved sun-dried tomatoes. Pull the parsley leaves from the stems and chop the leaves, reserving a few sprigs for garnish.

When the spaghetti is cooked, drain it in a colander. Add the reserved olive oil to the pan so the pasta does not stick. Return the pasta to the pan, add the olive purée and chopped parsley and toss until the spaghetti is thoroughly coated. Adjust the seasoning — the olives and tomatoes will almost certainly have contributed enough salt, but you may want to add some pepper or more red pepper flakes.

Pile the spaghetti in a warm serving bowl. Sprinkle it with the reserved olives, capers, sun-dried tomato shreds and parsley sprigs and serve at once.

RECAP

1 BRING LARGE COVERED PAN OF SALTED WATER TO BOIL. ALLOW 5-10 MINUTES FOR THIS.

2 ADD SPAGHETTI, STIR AND LEAVE TO SIMMER 8-10 MINUTES. MEANWHILE, PEEL GARLIC CLOVES AND ADD TO PROCESSOR WITH THREE-QUARTERS OF OLIVES, SUN-DRIED TOMATOES AND DRAINED CAPERS.

3 ADD PEPPER FLAKES TO PROCESSOR WITH OIL, RESERVING 1 TABLESPOON. WORK TO SMOOTH PURÉE. SET ASIDE.

4 SHRED RESERVED SUN-DRIED TOMATOES. CHOP PARSLEY LEAVES, RESERVING FEW SPRIGS FOR GARNISH.

5 WHEN SPAGHETTI IS COOKED 'AL DENTE', DRAIN

AND ADD RESERVED OIL TO PAN. POUR SPAGHETTI BACK INTO PAN. ADD OLIVE PURÉE AND CHOPPED PARSLEY AND TOSS UNTIL WELL MIXED.

6 ADJUST SEASONING, PILE IN WARM BOWL AND SPRINKLE WITH RESERVED OLIVES, CAPERS, TOMATO SHREDS AND PARSLEY SPRIGS.

See pages 2-3

TAGLIATELLE WITH CORIANDER & GINGER

TIME IN KITCHEN
14 minutes

serves 4

With its Oriental and Mexican connections, fresh coriander is also known as Chinese parsley and cilantro. Now the herb has invaded European tables with great success, valued for its aniseed flavour and ability to grow in most climates. Here it forms a brisk trio with lime and fresh ginger, a combination usually found with fish but why not with other ingredients like fresh pasta? The recipe could hardly be quicker to assemble — in fact the water takes longer to boil than the flavourings do to prepare. I'm suggesting you serve the pasta with a slice or two of smoked salmon as the flavourings complement it so well.

2 walnut-sized pieces of fresh ginger
large bunch of fresh coriander (about 60 g / 2 oz)
500 g / 1 lb fresh tagliatelle
2 limes
5 tablespoons olive oil
½ teaspoon ground white pepper, or more if needed
4 slices of smoked salmon (about 175 g / 6 oz)
salt

Put a large covered pot of salted water on to heat to bring to the boil, allowing 5-10 minutes for this before you start the recipe.

Start by thinly slicing the ginger with a large knife. There's no need to peel it, but do look carefully to see which way the fibres run — slicing first across the fibres makes the ginger much easier to chop. Lay the slices on the board and smash each one with the flat of the knife. Pull them together with the knife and finely chop them.

For the coriander, strip the leaves from the stems and chop the leaves with a large knife. I like to leave them quite coarse so as to add a bit of texture to the pasta, but it will have a more even colour if you chop them finer.

By now the water should be boiling. Add the tagliatelle, stirring to separate the strands. Bring to the boil again, then simmer for 1-2 minutes, stirring the tagliatelle occasionally.

Grate the zest from the limes, using a fine grater. To avoid having to brush zest from the grater, one trick is to stretch a piece of plastic film across the grid then grate as usual: the zest will be caught on the film. Sounds odd but it works. Squeeze the juice from one lime — we won't need the other one.

The best test for cooking pasta is to taste it — a strand should be firm to your bite. Drain it in a colander. Wipe out the pan, then return it to the heat and add the olive oil. Add the chopped ginger and sauté it for about a minute, until it is fragrant. Put back the tagliatelle with the coriander and lime zest and toss vigorously over the heat for about a minute, until the pasta is very hot and coated with oil.

Add the lime juice, white pepper and a little salt, toss well and taste for seasoning. Pile the tagliatelle on warmed individual plates with a slice of smoked salmon and serve at once.

RECAP

1 BRING LARGE COVERED PAN OF SALTED WATER TO BOIL, ALLOWING 5-10 MINUTES FOR THIS.

2 THINLY SLICE GINGER, CRUSH WITH FLAT OF KNIFE AND FINELY CHOP. PULL CORIANDER LEAVES FROM STEMS AND COARSELY CHOP.

3 WHEN WATER BOILS, ADD TAGLIATELLE, STIR AND COOK 1-2 MINUTES UNTIL JUST 'AL DENTE'.

4 MEANWHILE, GRATE ZEST FROM LIMES AND SQUEEZE JUICE FROM 1 LIME.

5 DRAIN PASTA. HEAT OLIVE OIL IN PAN AND SAUTÉ GINGER ABOUT 1 MINUTE.

PUT BACK PASTA WITH CORIANDER AND LIME ZEST. TOSS OVER HEAT FOR ABOUT 1 MINUTE.

6 ADD LIME JUICE, PEPPER AND LITTLE SALT. TOSS WELL AND ADJUST SEASONING. SERVE AT ONCE WITH A SLICE OF SMOKED SALMON.

SPEEDY SALADS

Because they involve preparing a multiplicity of vegetables, many salads are not speedy at all. So our first principle must be to look for recipes with at most three or four main ingredients, such as the Wilted Frisée & Bacon Salad, or Panzanella. Using ham, prawns or other meats and fish which come already cooked is also time-saving. The pungent flavour of cheese is a boon, as is the saltiness of anchovy and olives, and the zest of spring onions and garlic.

Next, beware of any single ingredient that takes a long time to prepare – even a head of lettuce takes about 3 minutes to trim, wash and dry thoroughly. So greens which need little more than a rinse – such as chicory, radicchio, celery, cabbage and bok-choy – are favourites. At a pinch, a packet of pre-washed gourmet greens can save the day, much as I deplore their price and mediocre quality.

There isn't time to hard-boil and shell eggs, and certainly we can't embark on skinning tomatoes or chopping more than one or two onions. So be prepared for the hearty old-fashioned textures of vegetables with peel and seeds, for the crunch of blanched cabbage and lightly cooked peppers. Flavours will be vivid and fresh, as there's little time for ingredients to marinate and mellow. One step must never be omitted, however – that of tasting the salad after tossing with dressing. Getting the right balance of flavours is essential.

left SWEET PEPPERS WITH PEPPERONI & ROCKET *see page 70*

SWEET PEPPERS WITH PEPPERONI & ROCKET

TIME IN KITCHEN
  14 minutes
STANDING *30 minutes if*
  possible
STORAGE *up to 24 hours*
  in the refrigerator
serves 4

2 large red peppers
2 large green peppers
2 large yellow peppers
125 ml / 4 fl oz olive oil
2 bunches of rocket
2 garlic cloves
250 g / ½ lb sliced
  pepperoni sausage
20 g / ⅔ oz capers
3 tablespoons red wine
  vinegar, or more if
  needed
salt and freshly ground
  black pepper

wok and stirrer

I first tasted this salad on a hot summer day in Italy, when I enjoyed a perfect lunch of sweet peppers, spicy sausage and bitter greens — with a sorbet and 'doppio espresso' to follow. It has never tasted quite the same at home — how could it without bulbous, vine-ripened peppers warm from the sun, not to mention the local butcher's pepperoni? Still, the mix here is remarkably effective. Be sure to buy the best pepperoni and have it sliced for you at the deli. With the addition of some scrambled eggs, this salad makes a delicious dish for brunch.

Halve the peppers and snap out the cores with your hands. Discard the seeds and cut each pepper half into 5 or 6 strips. You won't have to spend time on removing ribs from inside, but if they are very fleshy you may need to scoop them out with the knife.

Place the wok over a high heat for 15 seconds. Drizzle the oil around the sides and continue heating for 5 seconds more until very hot. Stir in the peppers with salt and pepper and toss and stir until very hot, about 1 minute. Leave them to cook over a high flame, stirring occasionally. We want the peppers to soften and to brown in one or two places — this will take a total of 6-9 minutes.

Meanwhile, trim off the rocket stems and wash the leaves in a sink full of cold water, stirring with your hands to loosen grit. Lift them out with your hands and dry on a towel or in a salad spinner.

Lightly crush the garlic cloves with the flat of the knife and discard the skin. With the flat of the knife, smash the cloves, then chop them with the blade. Stir the garlic into the peppers and continue frying for 2-3 minutes. When the peppers are cooked, stir in the sausage and leave over a low heat for 1 minute to allow the flavours to blend.

Drain the capers, rinse under cold running water and add to the pan of peppers together with the vinegar. Take from the heat, stir the salad thoroughly, taste and adjust the seasoning — the oil from cooking forms a dressing with the vinegar.

You can eat the salad at this stage if you like, but it will be much improved if left to marinate for about half an hour at room temperature.

To serve: arrange a semi-circle of rocket leaves on 4 individual plates. Taste and adjust the seasoning again as the balance may have changed as the dish cools. Pile the salad on the plates.

RECAP

1 HALVE PEPPERS, SNAP OUT CORES AND DISCARD SEEDS. CUT EACH HALF IN 5-6 STRIPS.

2 HEAT OIL IN WOK, STIR IN PEPPERS WITH SALT AND PEPPER AND LEAVE TO FRY BRISKLY UNTIL JUST TENDER AND BROWNED IN PLACES, 6-9 MINUTES TOTAL.

3 MEANWHILE, WASH AND DRY ROCKET. PEEL AND CHOP GARLIC AND STIR INTO PEPPERS. CONTINUE COOKING 2-3 MINUTES.

4 STIR SAUSAGE INTO PEPPERS AND LEAVE TO COOK 1 MINUTE.

5 DRAIN CAPERS, RINSE WITH COLD WATER AND ADD TO PEPPERS WITH VINEGAR.

6 TAKE SALAD FROM HEAT, STIR AND ADJUST SEASONING. IF TIME, LEAVE SALAD TO MARINATE FOR HALF HOUR AT ROOM TEMPERATURE.

7 TASTE SALAD AND ADJUST SEASONING AGAIN. ARRANGE WITH ROCKET LEAVES ON 4 INDIVIDUAL PLATES.

CRAZY SALAD

TIME IN KITCHEN
14 minutes

serves 4

It's hard to believe that in the days of nouvelle cuisine, *main-course salads were a novelty. Most of the hundreds of new salad combinations that appeared then have died a natural death — however, this apparently crazy recipe triumphantly survives.*

It invites ingredients of your choice: you can go upmarket with foie gras and lobster instead of chicken livers and shrimps; or substitute raspberries or mandarin orange segments (the '70s choice) for the mango; or use more delicate mixed salad greens instead of the cos. The only rule is to maintain the basic proportions of the salad, and to use nut oil and a fruit vinegar in the dressing.

1 large head of cos lettuce (about 500 g / 1 lb)
1 mango
125 g / 4 oz peeled cooked baby prawns
125 g / 4 oz chicken livers
60 g / 2 oz walnut pieces

for the dressing:
4 tablespoons raspberry or sherry vinegar
125 ml / 4 fl oz walnut oil
salt and freshly ground black pepper

Trim the lettuce stem and pull off the leaves, discarding any tough or damaged outer leaves. Immerse the leaves in a sink full of cold water and stir them with your hands to loosen grit. Lift them out with your hands so any grit is left behind, and spin them dry in a salad spinner or roll them in a tea towel. Arrange the small inner leaves around 4 individual plates. Bunch the larger leaves together on a chopping board and cut them across into coarse shreds, called a chiffonnade. Put them in a bowl ready to be tossed with dressing.

To prepare the mango: ripe mangoes are notoriously messy, so have a small bowl ready for the prepared fruit and work near the sink. With a small knife, cut the peel from the flesh. Inside the flesh is a large oval stone. Slice the flesh from the stone — inevitably the slices will be rough. Cut them into dice and put them in the bowl.

Make the dressing: whisk half of the vinegar in a small bowl with salt and pepper. Whisk in all but 2 tablespoons of the oil, adding it gradually so the dressing emulsifies and thickens slightly. Adjust the seasoning.

Add the prawns to the dressing and stir to mix. Add this to the shredded lettuce and stir until well coated. Taste a coated shred of lettuce, add more seasoning if necessary and pile the shredded lettuce and prawns on each plate. Scatter the mango dice on top.

Gently heat the remaining oil in a small frying pan. Cut the chicken livers into 3 or 4 slices, discarding any membrane, and sprinkle them with salt and pepper. Add them to the hot oil and fry over a high heat for 1-2 minutes, stirring so they cook on all sides. The outsides should be brown, but the insides still pink. Add the remaining vinegar and cook for about 15 seconds, stirring so the sticky juices on the bottom of the pan are dissolved in the vinegar — this gives a pleasant tang to the livers.

Spoon the livers over the salad, sprinkle with the walnut pieces and serve at once while the livers are still warm.

RECAP

1 WASH AND DRY LETTUCE, DISCARDING TOUGH OUTER LEAVES. ARRANGE SMALL LEAVES ON 4 INDIVIDUAL PLATES. COARSELY SHRED LARGER LEAVES AND PUT IN BOWL.

2 PEEL MANGO WITH SMALL KNIFE, CUT FLESH FROM STONE AND DICE.

3 MAKE VINAIGRETTE WITH HALF VINEGAR, SALT, PEPPER AND ALL BUT 2 TABLESPOONS OF OIL.

4 ADD PRAWNS TO DRESSING AND STIR TO MIX. ADD TO SHREDDED LETTUCE AND STIR UNTIL WELL COATED. TASTE LETTUCE SHRED, ADJUST SEASONING AND PILE ON EACH PLATE. SCATTER MANGO DICE ON TOP.

5 GENTLY HEAT REMAINING OIL IN SMALL FRYING PAN. CUT CHICKEN LIVERS IN 3-4 SLICES, DISCARDING MEMBRANE. ADD LIVERS TO HOT OIL AND FRY OVER HIGH HEAT 1-2 MINUTES, STIRRING SO THEY BROWN EVENLY. THEY SHOULD REMAIN PINK IN CENTRE. ADD REMAINING VINEGAR AND COOK ABOUT 15 SECONDS, STIRRING TO DEGLAZE PAN.

6 SPOON LIVERS ON TOP OF SALAD, SPRINKLE WITH WALNUT PIECES AND SERVE AT ONCE WHILE STILL WARM.

PANZANELLA

TIME IN KITCHEN
    10 minutes
STORAGE up to 1 hour
    at room temperature

serves 4

'Panzanella!' *said friends of ours who live in Tuscany. 'You need the ripest of tomatoes, the crispest of cucumbers, the most aromatic of basil, the fruitiest of oil and the sweetest of vinegar. It's all in our garden and kitchen.' So when we went to stay in their house one summer, we eagerly tackled the promised treat. And a treat indeed* panzanella *proved, full of fresh flavours and given body but lightness by the rustic local bread. The name* panzanella *means 'little swamp', as the bread soaks up dressing like marshy soil. I've found that many bakeries sell cut-price day-old bread — it works just fine!*

We always ate our panzanella *with Tuscan prosciutto, a drier and more gamy version of the familiar moist ham from Parma, which I suggest here. Any sliced country ham would be good, too.*

1 medium cucumber
750 g / 1½ lb very ripe
    beefsteak tomatoes
2 mild red onions
500 g / 1 lb loaf of
    ciabatta or crusty
    country bread
250-375 g / ½ - ¾ lb
    prosciutto

for the dressing:
1 garlic clove
3 tablespoons balsamic
    vinegar, or more to
    taste
4 tablespoons olive oil,
    or more to taste
large bunch of fresh
    basil
salt and freshly ground
    black pepper

First make the dressing: with the flat of the knife, lightly crush the garlic clove to loosen the skin and discard it. Smash the clove, then chop it with the knife blade. Put it in a small bowl. Whisk in the vinegar, salt and pepper. Gradually whisk in the oil until it emulsifies and thickens slightly.

Pull the leaves from the basil, roll them loosely and cut them into shreds, reserving 4 sprigs for decoration. If chopped too finely, they become bruised and bitter. Add the chopped basil to the dressing.

Peel the cucumber, cut it in half lengthwise and scoop out the seeds with a teaspoon or the end of the vegetable peeler. Cut the halves again lengthwise into 3 or 4 strips, then cut these across into small dice. We want the cucumber to add crunch, but it should not be too chunky.

Scoop out the tomato cores with a small knife, then cut the tomatoes into 8-16 wedges, depending on size. Cut each wedge into 2 or 3 pieces about double the size of the cucumber dice. You'll be glad to know that there's no need to peel the tomatoes.

To chop the onions: peel them, leaving a little of the root. Cut the onions in half through root and stem and set the cut sides down on a cutting board. Slice horizontally towards the root in parallel slices, cutting almost but not quite through the root. Slice vertically, again not cutting through the root so the slices are held together. Finally cut crosswise so the onion falls into dice. If they are not fine enough, chop them.

Cut the bread into 2.5 cm / 1 in cubes and set aside. Be sure to include the crust for body and colour.

Combine the cucumber, tomato and onion in a large bowl. Toss with the dressing. Add the bread cubes and toss to mix — they will soak up the dressing like a sponge. Leave for 5 minutes to allow the flavours to develop.

Meanwhile, arrange the prosciutto on 4 individual plates. It looks best when lightly pleated at one side of the plate, but don't be tempted to do this in advance as the ham will dry out within a few minutes.

Sprinkle the panzanella generously with black pepper — it must be freshly ground for maximum aroma. Taste the salad and adjust the seasoning, adding more oil, vinegar or salt if you like. Pile it on the plates, top with a basil sprig and serve within the hour to enjoy the fresh herb and vegetable flavours. Panzanella is best at room temperature.

1 MAKE DRESSING: PEEL AND CHOP GARLIC AND PUT IN SMALL BOWL. PULL LEAVES FROM BASIL AND CUT INTO SHREDS, RESERVING 4 SPRIGS FOR DECORATION. ADD BASIL SHREDS TO DRESSING.

2 PEEL CUCUMBER, SCOOP OUT SEEDS. CUT INTO LENGTHWISE STRIPS AND THEN INTO SMALL DICE.

3 CUT TOMATO INTO WEDGES AND CUT WEDGES INTO 2-3 PIECES.

4 CUT ONION INTO SMALL DICE AND COMBINE WITH CUCUMBERS AND TOMATOES. STIR IN DRESSING.

5 CUT BREAD INTO 2.5 CM / 1 IN CUBES, ADD TO SALAD AND TOSS TO MIX. LEAVE 5 MINUTES FOR FLAVOURS TO DEVELOP.

6 MEANWHILE, ARRANGE PROSCIUTTO ON 4 INDIVIDUAL PLATES.

7 SPRINKLE PANZANELLA WITH PEPPER. ADD MORE OIL, VINEGAR AND SALT TO TASTE AND PILE ON PLATES. TOP EACH WITH BASIL SPRIG.

BURGUNDIAN GREEK SALAD

TIME IN KITCHEN
12 minutes
STANDING *1-2 hours, if possible*
STORAGE *up to 24 hours in the refrigerator*

serves 4

I couldn't resist this contradictory title as it sums up one of our favourite summer salads. The essentials of a typical Greek salad are very simple — tomatoes, sweet onions, cucumbers and peppers, mixed with Feta cheese and Kalamata oil-cured black olives. In this Burgundian adaptation, we begin with the abundant juicy baby tomatoes and slightly bitter cucumbers from our garden, adding our local goats' cheese instead of Feta, fat black olives from Nyons in Provence and handfuls of home-grown herbs. All make for a salad of glowing fresh colours, the ingredients cut into large dice which are a feature of the presentation.

We also make our own vinegar, inspired by Elizabeth David who wrote one of the few helpful booklets on the subject. You need to start with a 'mother', the gelatinous membrane occasionally found in bottles of unpasteurized vinegar. Transfer it to an earthenware crock (darkness and warmth are important), feed it with two or three bottles of red wine and cover the top with a double layer of cheesecloth so that air can still circulate. After a month, taste the vinegar — it should be ready for use. From then on, as you draw off the vinegar, keep topping up with leftover red wine. Flavour will vary with the wine you add. It will also mellow with time and will be much more interesting than the commercial product.

This is a rustic salad, so don't even think of peeling tomatoes, thinly slicing cucumbers or stoning olives — crunchy chunks and chewy peel are quite in order. You can easily increase the quantities, though dealing with the vegetables will take a little longer. To make the salad go further, serve it on a bed of couscous, which takes almost no time to prepare.

**250 g / ½ lb cherry
 tomatoes**
2 medium cucumbers
2 green peppers
2 medium sweet onions
**500 g / 1 lb firm goats'
 cheese or Feta**
**150 g / 5 oz black oil-
 cured olives**
small bunch of basil
**small bunch of flat-leaf
 parsley**

for the dressing:
**3 tablespoons red wine
 vinegar**
125 ml / 4 fl oz olive oil
**salt and freshly ground
 black pepper**

Rinse the tomatoes in a colander under running water. Discard any stems and put them in a large bowl. Cut your cucumbers in half lengthwise and scoop out the seeds with a teaspoon or the end of the vegetable peeler. Cut the cucumber halves in 3 or 4 lengthwise strips, then cut these across into dice and add to the tomatoes. If the cucumbers have been waxed, you'll need to peel them first.

Halve the peppers, snap out the cores and discard the seeds. Cut the pepper halves lengthwise into 4 or 5 strips, then across into rough dice. Add to the tomatoes.

Peel the onions, leaving the root. Cut a thin slice from one side so the onion sits flat, then thinly slice it parallel to the 'equator', discarding the top. Push out the rings with your fingers, letting them fall into the bowl of vegetables.

Cut the cheese into dice and add to the vegetables together with the olives.

Make the dressing: whisk the vinegar with pepper and a little salt – the cheese and olives will add more salt. Gradually whisk in the oil so the dressing emulsifies and thickens slightly. Taste and adjust the seasoning.

Pour the dressing over the vegetables. Stir gently but thoroughly with two spoons – if the ingredients fall apart a bit, don't worry, their flavours will mix all the more. Taste the salad and adjust the seasoning again.

Finally, pull the herb leaves from the stems and chop them very coarsely – some texture will suit the salad. Add them to the other ingredients, mix gently and taste one last time. The salad can certainly be served at once, but flavours will mellow if you leave it an hour or two.

RECAP

1 *RINSE AND DRAIN TOMATOES, DISCARDING STEMS, AND PUT IN LARGE BOWL. CUT CUCUMBERS IN HALF LENGTHWISE, SCOOP OUT SEEDS AND CUT EACH HALF INTO 3-4 STRIPS. CUT FLESH IN DICE AND ADD TO TOMATOES.*

2 *HALVE PEPPERS AND DISCARD CORES AND SEEDS. CUT HALVES INTO STRIPS, THEN ACROSS INTO DICE. ADD TO TOMATOES.*

3 *PEEL ONIONS, THINLY SLICE ACROSS 'EQUATOR' AND SEPARATE SLICES INTO RINGS. ADD TO OTHER VEGETABLES.*

4 *DICE CHEESE AND ADD TO VEGETABLES WITH OLIVES.*

5 *MAKE VINAIGRETTE DRESSING WITH VINEGAR, SALT, PEPPER AND OIL. ADJUST SEASONING.*

6 *MIX DRESSING THOROUGHLY WITH VEGETABLES, TASTE AND ADJUST SEASONING AGAIN.*

7 *COARSELY CHOP HERB LEAVES, MIX GENTLY WITH SALAD AND TASTE ONE LAST TIME. SALAD CAN BE SERVED AT ONCE, BUT IS BETTER CHILLED FOR HOUR OR TWO.*

WARM PROVENÇAL SALAD OF FRESH TUNA

TIME IN KITCHEN
12 minutes

serves 4

4 boneless tuna steaks
(about 625 g / 1¼ lb
in total)
500 g / 1 lb macaroni
125 g / 4 oz black
Niçoise olives
8 anchovy fillets
few leaves of lettuce or
spinach, or sprigs of
watercress
500 g / 1 lb cherry
tomatoes
for the dressing:
2 garlic cloves
2 lemons
1 teaspoon dried
thyme
2 teaspoons Dijon-style
mustard
175 ml / 6 fl oz olive oil
salt and pepper

Inspired by the classic Salade Niçoise, *this warm pasta salad has many of the same ingredients — but with a twist. The tuna is freshly grilled instead of from a can, and quickly cooked pasta takes the place of potatoes. If you can't find the tiny brine-cured olives from Nice, substitute any black olives with a good flavour. When in a real rush you could substitute canned for fresh tuna.*

Preheat the grill. Bring a large pan of salted water to the boil for the pasta, covering with the lid so it boils more quickly. Allow 5-10 minutes for this before you start.

Make the dressing: lightly crush the garlic cloves with the flat of a knife to loosen the skin and discard. Smash the cloves, chop and put in a small bowl. Squeeze the juice from the lemons and add to the garlic with the thyme, mustard, salt and pepper. Gradually whisk in the oil so it thickens slightly and emulsifies. Adjust the seasoning.

Stir the pasta into the boiling water, bring back to the boil and simmer for 5-7 minutes, until the pasta is tender but still 'al dente' — chewy when you taste a piece.

Meanwhile, brush both sides of the tuna steaks with dressing and set them on the grill rack. Grill them 5 cm / 2 in from the heat for about 2 minutes until browned.

Meanwhile, chop the anchovies and stir them into the remaining dressing. Turn the tuna steaks and brown the other sides: allowing 1-2 minutes if you like your tuna rare in the centre, or 2-3 minutes if you prefer it better done. In any case, a translucent line should remain in the centre when you test it by poking with a small knife.

While the tuna finishes cooking, rinse the lettuce or greens in a colander under cold water and dry on paper towels. Arrange them around a large bowl.

When the tuna is cooked, remove it from the grill and set aside. Test the pasta. When cooked, drain it and return it to the pan. Add the dressing with the olives and toss with two large forks. Taste, adding more thyme, mustard, salt or pepper.

Pile the pasta salad in the bowl, set the tuna steaks on top and arrange the tomatoes around the edge. Serve while still warm.

RECAP

1 PREHEAT GRILL. BRING LARGE COVERED PAN OF SALTED WATER TO BOIL. ALLOW 5-10 MINUTES.

2 MAKE DRESSING: CHOP GARLIC. PUT IT IN SMALL BOWL WITH THE JUICE FROM LEMONS, THYME, MUSTARD, SALT AND PEPPER. GRADUALLY WHISK IN OIL SO IT EMULSIFIES. TASTE AND ADJUST SEASONING.

3 STIR PASTA INTO BOILING WATER, BRING BACK TO BOIL AND SIMMER 5-7 MINUTES UNTIL 'AL DENTE'.

4 MEANWHILE, BRUSH BOTH SIDES OF STEAKS WITH DRESSING AND SET ON GRILL RACK. GRILL ABOUT 5 CM / 2 IN FROM HEAT ABOUT 2 MINUTES UNTIL BROWN. TURN STEAKS AND BROWN OTHER SIDES, 1-2 MINUTES FOR RARE OR 2-3 FOR BETTER DONE.

5 MEANWHILE, CHOP ANCHOVIES AND STIR INTO REMAINING DRESSING. RINSE AND DRY GREENS, AND ARRANGE IN LARGE BOWL.

6 WHEN TUNA IS COOKED, REMOVE FROM GRILL AND SET ASIDE.

7 DRAIN PASTA AND RETURN TO PAN. ADD DRESSING WITH OLIVES, TOSS TO MIX, TASTE AND ADJUST SEASONING.

8 PILE SALAD INTO BOWL. SET TUNA ON TOP AND ARRANGE TOMATOES AROUND. SERVE WARM.

SCALLOP SALAD WITH CUMIN DRESSING

TIME IN KITCHEN
  10 minutes
CHILLING at least
  1 hour in the
  refrigerator
STORAGE up to 24 hours
  in the refrigerator

serves 4

625 g / 1¼ lb scallops
250 ml / 8 fl oz dry
  white wine
2-3 sprigs of thyme
1 bay leaf
1 large head of
  butterhead lettuce
  or 2 heads of Little
  Gem
3 spring onions
4 plum tomatoes

for the dressing:
2 tablespoons sherry
  vinegar or red wine
  vinegar
1 tablespoon ground
  cumin
1 teaspoon crushed
  dried hot red chilli
  pepper
5 tablespoons walnut
  or olive oil
salt and freshly ground
  black pepper

This unexpected mix of scallops, spring onions and tomato, spiced with cumin and chilli, is one of those inspired combinations which are quite simple but just right. Spring onions give texture, tomatoes sweetness, cumin underlines the delicacy of the scallops, while the chilli prevents them from being bland.

Look for plump, fresh-smelling scallops with a minimum of liquid — allow 3-5 per person (big ones will come about 10 to the 500 g / 1 lb). One of my own personal time-savers is to use plum tomatoes for salad. They have such thin skins that I don't bother peeling them.

With generous amounts of lettuce, I think you'll find the scallops a satisfying main course, but if you want more substance add some small potatoes boiled in their jackets and served warm, tossed in more of the dressing.

Start by poaching the scallops: put 375 ml / 12 fl oz water in a medium saucepan with the wine, thyme and bay leaf. Bring to the boil and leave to simmer.

Meanwhile, drain the scallops and add any juice to the poaching liquid. Remove the tough crescent-shaped muscle from the side of each scallop. Add them to the poaching liquid and bring just back to a simmer, stirring so they cook evenly. Take from the heat and leave the scallops to stand in the liquid. They cook very quickly, so this brief time is enough. If they overcook they will be dry and tough.

Trim the lettuce, separate the leaves and immerse them in a sink full of cold water, shaking them with your hands to loosen grit. Lift them out, dry them in a salad spin-ner or roll them in a tea towel and put them to chill in the refrigerator. I often keep salad overnight this way — it stays moist and the cold crisps the leaves.

Make the dressing: whisk the vinegar with the cumin, chilli pepper, salt and black pepper in a medium bowl until mixed. Gradually whisk in the oil so the dressing emul-sifies and thickens slightly. Taste and adjust the seasoning.

Trim the spring onions and cut them across at an angle into 1 cm / ⅜ in slices. Add them to the dressing. Core the tomatoes, cut them across in half and squeeze out the seeds. Cut the flesh into small cubes and add them to the dressing.

Drain the scallops and discard the thyme and bay leaf. Keep the cooking liquid as this is excellent stock for poaching fish or the basis for a sauce. It freezes well.

Add the scallops to the dressing and mix the salad thoroughly with two spoons. Cover and leave it to chill at least an hour.

Just before serving, arrange the lettuce leaves on 4 individual plates. Taste the scal-lops and adjust the seasoning, then pile them on the lettuce leaves.

PRAWN & SQUID SALAD WITH CORIANDER DRESSING

With prawns and squid instead of scallops, and a flavouring of coriander, the salad given above becomes typically Italian. Substitute 250 g / ½ lb cooked peeled prawns and 500 g / 1 lb raw cleaned baby squid for the scallops. Wash and dry the squid. Cut the tentacles from the body sacs, leaving them joined. Cut the body sacs into rings. Simmer the squid as for the scallops. Make the dressing as described, substituting coriander for the cumin. Drain the squid, mix with the prawns and finish the salad as described.

RECAP

1 POACH SCALLOPS: PUT 375 ML / 12 FL OZ WATER IN MEDIUM SAUCEPAN, WITH WINE, THYME AND BAY LEAF. LEAVE TO SIMMER.

2 DRAIN JUICES FROM SCALLOPS AND ADD TO POACHING LIQUID. DISCARD CRESCENT-SHAPED MUSCLES FROM SCALLOPS AND ADD THEM TO POACHING LIQUID. BRING JUST TO SIMMER AND SET ASIDE OFF HEAT.

3 TRIM LETTUCE, DIVIDE LEAVES, WASH AND DRY. KEEP IN REFRIGERATOR.

4 MAKE VINAIGRETTE DRESSING WITH VINEGAR, CUMIN, CHILLI PEPPER AND OIL. TASTE AND ADJUST SEASONING.

5 TRIM AND DIAGONALLY SLICE SPRING ONIONS. ADD TO DRESSING. CORE TOMATOES, HALVE AND SQUEEZE OUT SEEDS. DICE TOMATOES AND ADD TO DRESSING.

6 DRAIN SCALLOPS, DISCARDING THYME AND BAY LEAF (KEEP FISH STOCK FOR ANOTHER USE).

7 ADD SCALLOPS TO DRESSING AND MIX WELL. CHILL AT LEAST 1 HOUR.

8 TO FINISH: ARRANGE LETTUCE LEAVES ON 4 INDIVIDUAL PLATES. TASTE AND ADJUST SALAD SEASONING AND PILE ON LEAVES.

SALAD OF FIG-STUFFED CHICKEN WITH BLUE CHEESE

TIME IN KITCHEN
11 minutes
BAKING *30-35 minutes*

serves 4

Combining chicken with dried fruit and blue cheese sounds odd, but be assured that this recipe is greater than the sum of its parts. As you might expect, it comes from California and was originally designed for Mission figs (a particularly intensely flavoured variety), and the best Maytag blue cheese. The chicken can be served warm or cold, set on a leafy bed of peppery greens such as rocket, watercress or radicchio. For more people, it takes little more time to fill some extra chicken breasts.

Perhaps this is the place to talk about salad greens — tough or tender, peppery or mild. Salad leaves almost always act as the background to a salad rather than the lead ingredient, so can be changed without affecting the basic character of the salad itself. Don't hesitate to swap spinach for butterhead lettuce or an economical head of cos for expensive chicory. Make a choice from what you like best (that's the cook's privilege) and what looks tempting in the market on that particular day.

4 boneless chicken
   breasts
15 g / ½ oz butter
1 spring onion
60 g / 2 oz mushrooms
1 slice of white bread
15 g / ½ oz blue cheese
30 g / 1 oz dried figs
salt and freshly ground
   black pepper

for the salad:
small bunch of rocket
small head of radicchio

for the dressing:
1 teaspoon Dijon-style
   mustard
2 tablespoons red wine
   vinegar
125 ml / 4 fl oz olive oil

food processor

Preheat the oven to 190°C/375°F/gas5 — allow 5 minutes for this before you start.

Butter a medium baking dish. Heat the remaining butter in a medium frying pan. While it melts, trim the spring onion, cut it across at an angle into 1 cm / ⅜ in slices and add to the butter. Cook over a low heat for 1-2 minutes until slightly soft.

Meanwhile, trim the mushroom stems and wipe the caps with a damp cloth. If they are very sandy you may need to rinse them in cold water. Cut them into 2 or 3 pieces. Put these in the food processor and finely chop, using the pulse button. Be careful, as mushrooms are full of water and if over-chopped they will turn to liquid.

Stir the mushrooms into the spring onion, add salt and pepper and leave to cook over a quite high heat. The heat will draw out the mushroom liquid, so keep cooking for 2-3 minutes until it evaporates.

Meanwhile, tear the slice of bread into 2 or 3 pieces, add to the processor and work to fine crumbs. Crumble the blue cheese into a bowl with your fingers. With a knife, trim the figs and chop them.

When the liquid has evaporated from the mushrooms, take the pan from the heat and stir in the breadcrumbs, cheese and figs. Add pepper and taste the stuffing for seasoning before adding salt as the cheese may be salty enough.

Discard any skin from the chicken breasts. With a small sharp knife, cut a horizontal pocket, working the whole length of the breast and being careful not to cut all the way through. Divide the stuffing evenly among the pockets, pushing it inside as far as possible with a spoon.

Set the chicken breasts in the buttered baking dish and sprinkle them with salt and pepper. Cover tightly with foil and bake in the oven for 30-35 minutes. With the point of a knife, cut into the centre of the largest breast — the meat should be thoroughly cooked, with no pink juices running. If necessary, bake for another 5-10 minutes.

Make the salad: rinse the rocket under cold running water, shake to dry the leaves and trim the stems. Trim off the stem of the radicchio, discard any wilted outer leaves and cut the head across into coarse shreds, called a chiffonnade. Put the leaves in a bowl while you make the salad dressing.

Put the mustard in a small bowl with salt and pepper. Whisk in the vinegar. Add the oil in a slow steady stream, whisking constantly so the dressing emulsifies and thickens slightly, helped by the mustard. Taste and adjust the seasoning.

To finish: if serving the chicken hot, slice the breasts as soon as they are cooked. However, you will find they are easier to slice when cold. Cut each one into 4 or 5 diagonal slices. Slide the knife under the slices and transfer them to 4 individual plates, fanning them out on half of the plate to show the coloured stuffing.

Add about half the dressing to the salad, toss to mix and taste a leaf. Adjust the seasoning again if necessary. Pile the salad on the plates. Spoon the remaining dressing over the chicken to moisten it.

RECAP

1 PREHEAT OVEN TO 190°C/375°F/GAS5 — ALLOW 5 MINUTES FOR THIS BEFORE YOU START.

2 BUTTER MEDIUM BAKING DISH. MELT REMAINING BUTTER IN FRYING PAN. SLICE SPRING ONION DIAGONALLY, ADD TO BUTTER AND LEAVE TO SOFTEN OVER LOW HEAT.

3 TRIM AND WIPE MUSHROOMS AND CUT INTO 2-3 PIECES. CHOP IN FOOD PROCESSOR AND ADD TO SPRING ONION WITH SALT AND PEPPER. LEAVE TO COOK OVER HIGH HEAT 2-3 MINUTES UNTIL THEIR LIQUID EVAPORATES.

4 WORK BREAD TO CRUMBS IN FOOD PROCESSOR. CRUMBLE BLUE CHEESE AND CHOP FIGS. WHEN MUSHROOMS ARE FAIRLY DRY, TAKE PAN FROM HEAT AND STIR IN BREADCRUMBS, CHEESE AND FIGS. SEASON STUFFING TO TASTE.

5 DISCARD ANY SKIN FROM CHICKEN BREASTS AND CUT POCKET IN EACH. FILL WITH STUFFING. SET BREASTS IN BUTTERED DISH. COVER WITH FOIL AND BAKE 30-35 MINUTES OR UNTIL NO PINK JUICE RUNS OUT WHEN CENTRE OF BIGGEST BREAST IS CUT INTO WITH KNIFE.

6 MAKE SALAD: WASH ROCKET. TRIM STEM OF RADICCHIO AND DISCARD ANY WILTED OUTER LEAVES. CUT HEAD ACROSS INTO STRIPS. MAKE DRESSING.

7 SERVE BREASTS HOT OR COLD, CUTTING THEM IN 4-5 DIAGONAL SLICES AND FANNING THEM ON ONE SIDE OF 4 INDIVIDUAL PLATES.

8 DRESS SALAD, RESERVING HALF DRESSING. PILE SALAD ON EACH PLATE AND SPOON REMAINING DRESSING OVER CHICKEN.

RED CABBAGE, APPLE & ROQUEFORT SALAD

TIME IN KITCHEN
10 minutes
STANDING *15 minutes*
STORAGE *up to 4 hours
in the refrigerator*

serves 4

½ **head of red cabbage
(about 500 g / 1 lb)**
**125 ml / 4 fl oz red
wine vinegar**
**1 large tart green
apple**
**75 g / 2½ oz Roquefort
cheese**

for the dressing:
**1 tablespoon Dijon-
style mustard**
**3 tablespoons red wine
vinegar**
**175 ml / 6 fl oz walnut
oil**
**salt and freshly ground
black pepper**

Even in the depths of winter, a head of red cabbage can be relied on to be crisp and colourful. It discolours easily, however, so from the start you must take precautions to preserve its vivid leaves. First, shred the cabbage with a stainless-steel blade — if you are adept with a vegetable mandoline, here's the place to use it; alternatively, employ a large chef's knife. Next, mix the cabbage with an acid ingredient to set the colour. In this recipe we're tossing the cabbage in hot red wine vinegar before mixing it with a tart green apple.

The other problem with red cabbage is its toughness — it is, after all, a winter plant. So a bath in boiling water is needed to wilt it before you add a dressing of walnut oil (the more flavour the better). By itself, the salad is a robust appetizer, or for a main course the peppery flavour of the cabbage is a natural with hot sausages or a topping of crispy bacon.

Bring a covered medium pan of water to the boil — allow 5-10 minutes for this before you start the recipe.

Meanwhile, shred the cabbage. First discard any wilted leaves, then cut out the central stem. If shredding by hand, set the cabbage cut side down on a board and slice across into the finest possible shreds, working at right angles to the stem. Discard any thick ribs and put the cabbage in a large bowl.

Bring the vinegar to the boil, standing well back as vapour from the vinegar will sting your eyes. Pour the vinegar over the cabbage and mix well. The cabbage will turn a dramatic bright red.

Remove the pan of boiling water from the heat, add the cabbage, cover and leave it for 2-3 minutes to soften.

Meanwhile, make the dressing: put the mustard in a small bowl with salt and pepper. Whisk in the vinegar. Add the oil in a slow steady stream, whisking constantly so the dressing emulsifies and thickens slightly, helped by the mustard.

Wipe the apple and scoop out stem and flower ends with a small knife. I like to leave the green skin for colour, but you can peel it if you prefer. Halve it and scoop out the core. To cut the apple quickly in rough chunks, set each cored half flat side down on a board. Cut across into 4 or 5 slices, turn the slices 90 degrees and cut them across 4 or 5 times to form chunks. Add the apples to the dressing and toss thoroughly so the cut surfaces do not discolour.

Drain the cabbage in a colander. Pat it dry with paper towels and replace it in the bowl. Add the apples and the dressing, mix everything well together and adjust the seasoning. Salads like this benefit from standing, so the strong flavours of cabbage, vinegar and walnut oil can marry; 15 minutes chilling in the refrigerator is a minimum, and up to 4 hours is even better.

Crumble the Roquefort cheese on top of the salad just before serving.

RED CABBAGE, APPLE & ROQUEFORT SALAD

RECAP

1 BRING COVERED MEDIUM PAN OF WATER TO BOIL. ALLOW 5-10 MINUTES FOR THIS BEFORE YOU START.

2 MEANWHILE, SHRED CABBAGE AND PUT IT IN LARGE BOWL. BRING VINEGAR TO BOIL, POUR OVER CABBAGE AND MIX WELL.

3 TAKE BOILING WATER FROM HEAT, ADD CABBAGE, COVER PAN AND LEAVE 2-3 MINUTES.

4 MAKE DRESSING: PUT MUSTARD IN SMALL BOWL WITH SALT AND PEPPER. WHISK IN VINEGAR, THEN OIL IN SLOW STEADY STREAM.

5 WIPE APPLE AND SCOOP OUT STEM AND FLOWER ENDS WITH SMALL KNIFE. HALVE APPLE, SCOOP OUT CORE AND CUT IN CHUNKS. ADD TO DRESSING AND TOSS.

6 DRAIN CABBAGE IN COLANDER. PAT DRY WITH PAPER TOWELS AND REPLACE IN BOWL. ADD APPLES AND DRESSING, MIX WELL AND ADJUST SEASONING. CHILL AT LEAST 15 MINUTES.

7 CRUMBLE CHEESE ON TOP JUST BEFORE SERVING.

WILTED FRISÉE
& BACON SALAD

TIME IN KITCHEN
8 minutes

serves 4

I always know when it is autumn in France because hot bacon salad makes its appearance on bistro menus. The hot bacon is not in deference to the cooler weather, but rather to the toughness of the seasonal greens — frisée, escarole and dandelion. The dressing of hot bacon fat, followed by boiling vinegar to dissolve the pan juices, effectively wilts all but the most fibrous green leaves (which in any case should be discarded in favour of the white inner fronds). In this recipe I've added a dash of Cognac to cut the bacon fat and raise the spirits. To make the salad a main course, add a hard-boiled egg or two.

**175 g / 6 oz thickly
sliced lean smoked
bacon**
**1 medium head of
frisée or escarole
(about 750 g / 1½ lb)**
1 tablespoon oil
**3 tablespoons red wine
vinegar**
3 tablespoons Cognac
**freshly ground black
pepper**

Trim any rind or bone from the bacon, then cut across the slices to make strips, called in French 'lardons'. Heat the oil with the lardons in a frying pan over a medium heat and fry until the fat is rendered and the bacon is beginning to brown.

Meanwhile, prepare the salad greens but stir the bacon occasionally and watch out that it does not burn. Trim the stem of the frisée or escarole. Pull off most of the green outside leaves and discard them as they are very tough. Pull apart the remaining white and pale green leaves. With luck, they will not need to be washed. If they are dirty, however, immerse them in a sink full of cold water and shake them with your hands to loosen grit. Lift them out with your hands, so grit is left behind. Dry the leaves in a salad spinner or roll them in a dry tea towel. Transfer them to a salad bowl and have two salad spoons ready.

Continue cooking the bacon until brown, even crispy if you like. If you have more than about 3 tablespoons of fat, discard some. Pour the hot fat and bacon over the salad greens and toss like mad so the leaves wilt and are evenly coated.

Put the pan back on the heat, add the vinegar and cook, stirring to dissolve the sticky juices on the bottom of the pan, until reduced by about half. Don't get too close or the vinegar vapour will sting your eyes.

Take the pan from the heat, add the Cognac and flame it by lighting with a match, again standing well back. If the Cognac does not light at once, put it back over the heat.

Pour this over the greens and toss again. Add freshly ground black pepper, taste and adjust the seasoning — remember the bacon is already salty so more is unlikely to be needed. Rush to the table.

RECAP

1 CUT BACON ACROSS INTO STRIPS. FRY IN OIL IN FRYING PAN UNTIL STARTING TO BROWN, STIRRING OCCASIONALLY.

2 MEANWHILE, SEPARATE FRISÉE OR ESCAROLE INTO LEAVES, DISCARDING TOUGH OUTER GREEN ONES. WASH LEAVES ONLY IF NECESSARY, DRYING WELL. PUT IN SALAD BOWL.

3 BROWN BACON, DISCARDING FAT IF YOU HAVE MORE THAN ABOUT 3 TABLESPOONS. POUR HOT FAT AND BACON OVER GREENS AND TOSS THOROUGHLY.

4 RETURN PAN TO HEAT, ADD VINEGAR AND REDUCE BY HALF, STIRRING TO DISSOLVE STICKY JUICES ON BOTTOM OF PAN.

5 TAKE FROM HEAT, ADD COGNAC AND FLAME.

6 POUR OVER GREENS AND TOSS AGAIN. ADD PEPPER, ADJUST SEASONING AND SERVE AT ONCE.

CHICORY SALAD WITH GOATS' CHEESE TOASTS

TIME IN KITCHEN
8 minutes
GRILLING 3-5 minutes

serves 4 as a first course

Ten years ago this recipe was virtually unknown, but it has since become a classic — a staple in bistros from Lyon to Los Angeles. What varies most is the salad leaf used and I often settle on chicory — it is expensive, but a little goes a long way. Better still, it is the easiest of leaves to prepare, needing only to be trimmed without washing. Watercress is almost as quick: a twist to remove the stems, a rinse in water and it's ready. As for the goats' cheese, it should be just soft enough to spread, so it melts and browns well.

With just one round of toasted cheese on bread per person as here, the salad is a first course; increase the number to three and it becomes my favourite summer lunch.

Dressed salads — with their oil and vinegar — are not the best companions for wine, but this recipe is redeemed by goats' cheese. An accompanying glass of red wine, such as a Beaujolais, is very much in order.

2 small goats' cheeses or 1 small log (about 175 g / 6 oz)
½ loaf of French bread
2 tablespoons stoned black or green olives
2 heads (about 375 g / ¾ lb) of chicory
large bunch of watercress
for the dressing:
1 teaspoon Dijon-style mustard
2 tablespoons raspberry or red wine vinegar
6 tablespoons olive oil
salt and freshly ground black pepper

Preheat the grill — allow 5 minutes for this before you start the recipe.

Make the dressing: whisk the mustard, salt and pepper with the vinegar in a small bowl until mixed. Gradually add the olive oil, whisking constantly so the dressing emulsifies and thickens slightly. Give it a first taste for seasoning.

Cut the goats' cheese into 4 rounds. Cut 4 rounds of bread about 1.25 cm / ½ in thick. Brush them with dressing so they brown nicely under the grill. Put them on a baking sheet. Slice or very coarsely chop the olives and spread them on the bread. Set a slice of cheese on top and brush with the dressing once more. If the bread is not completely covered with cheese, spread it to the edges with a knife or the bread will scorch.

Grill about 7.5 cm / 3 in from the heat until the cheese is melted and browned, about 3-5 minutes.

Meanwhile, wipe the chicory and trim the bases. Cut across into 2 cm / ¾ in diagonal slices and transfer to a large bowl.

Give a sharp twist to the bunch of watercress to break the stems. Immerse the leaves in cold water, lift them out with your hands, shake and dry them on a tea towel. Add them to the bowl. Add the dressing, toss with salad spoons and taste; you will almost certainly need more seasoning.

Pile the salad on four serving plates. The goats' cheese is ready when it has melted slightly and browned. Set a round of toast on each salad and serve at once.

RECAP

1 PREHEAT GRILL — ALLOW 5 MINUTES FOR THIS.

2 MAKE DRESSING: WHISK MUSTARD AND VINEGAR WITH SALT AND PEPPER IN SMALL BOWL UNTIL MIXED. GRADUALLY WHISK IN OIL, SO IT EMULSIFIES, AND ADJUST SEASONING.

3 CUT CHEESE INTO 4 ROUNDS AND CUT 4 ROUNDS OF BREAD. BRUSH BREAD WITH DRESSING, SET ON A BAKING SHEET. SLICE OR CHOP OLIVES AND SPREAD ON BREAD. TOP WITH CHEESE AND BRUSH AGAIN WITH DRESSING.

4 GRILL UNTIL MELTED AND BROWNED, 3-5 MINUTES.

5 WIPE CHICORY, TRIM AND CUT INTO 2 CM / ¾ IN DIAGONAL SLICES. PUT IN BOWL. TWIST STEMS OFF BUNCH OF WATERCRESS AND WASH LEAVES. DRY AND ADD TO CHICORY. TOSS WITH DRESSING AND ADJUST SEASONING. PILE ON 4 SERVING PLATES.

6 WHEN CHEESE IS TOASTED, SET A ROUND ON EACH SALAD AND SERVE.

ON THE LIGHT SIDE

I nearly called this chapter 'Vegetarian, but not Quite'. Some recipes are indeed vegetarian, and one or two (such as Provençal Tricolor and Roast Root Vegetables with Walnuts) are even vegan, but most rely on ham or bacon – or perhaps chicken stock – to bolster flavour. Several feature cheese in off-beat recipes like Frittata with Spinach & Goats' Cheese, and Blue Cheese Puff – a giant batter pudding. With their emphasis on vegetables, they are light as well as healthy and nutritious – and a complete meal in themselves.

We're all eating this way nowadays, whether for health reasons or, as in my case, for the pleasure of exploring the many different tastes and textures of vegetables and fruits. We can all profit from the revolution in year-round supplies, with exotica like okra, celeriac and even beansprouts now commonplace in many markets. The recipe for Roast Root Vegetables with Walnuts offers a chance to try out a new root such as salsify or Japanese artichoke. For that matter, any type of squash can take the place of pumpkin in Baked Pumpkin with Plums & Bacon.

So in this chapter I hope you'll embark on some experiments. Baked eggs can be flavoured with all sorts of vegetables besides spring onions, and a frittata begs for a filling of whatever vegetables you have to hand. Just be sure what you buy is fresh, preferably in season.

left BAKED PUMPKIN WITH PLUMS & BACON *see page 90*

BAKED PUMPKIN WITH PLUMS & BACON

TIME IN KITCHEN
   14 minutes
BAKING *50-60 minutes
   (10-12 in microwave)*
STORAGE *up to 2 days in
   the refrigerator*
serves 4

**250 g / ½ lb thickly
   sliced bacon**
100 g / 3½ oz butter
**500 g / 1 lb purple
   plums**
**1.4 kg / 3 lb pieces of
   pumpkin**
**1 tablespoon brown
   sugar**
**1 teaspoon ground
   cinnamon**
**1 teaspoon ground
   allspice**
½ teaspoon salt
**½ teaspoon freshly
   ground black pepper**

This recipe dates back to Colonial America, and is a good example of subsistence cooking in which ingredients which happen to be in season are combined almost at random.
The combination of pumpkin and plums is a happy one, married with salty bacon, sugar and spice. Such savoury and sweet combinations were also typical of the period. You may use other winter squash, such as butternut. The dish is good served with a grain pilaf or with grilled breast of duck or pork chops. Make double or triple quantity of the recipe, no problem!

Preheat the oven to 190°C/375°F/gas 5, allowing 5 minutes for this before you start.

Cut the bacon across into dice. Heat 15 g / ½ oz of the butter in a frying pan and sauté the bacon for 5-7 minutes over medium heat until browned and slightly crisp.

Meanwhile, halve the plums, cutting through the indentation and twisting to loosen them from the stone. Scoop the stone from the other half with a small knife. Freestone varieties of plum will loosen easily from the stone, but clingstones are more obstinate and unfortunately you cannot tell their type without testing. Put them in a large bowl.

Keep an eye on the bacon and butter. When the bacon is brown, add the remaining butter, turn the heat to low and leave the butter to melt in the hot fat.

Scrape the seeds and fibres from the pumpkin with a spoon. Set the pumpkin flat side down on a chopping board and, using a serrated knife, cut the skin down and away from the flesh. Take care, as pumpkin skin is tough and the knife can slip easily. Cut the pumpkin into wedges, then into 2.5 cm / 1 in cubes; they should weigh about 825 g / 1¾ lb in total. Some stores sell bags of ready-prepared pieces of pumpkin – snap them up. Add the pumpkin to the plums.

Stir the sugar, cinnamon, allspice, salt and pepper into the bacon and melted butter. Pour the mixture over the plums and pumpkin and stir with two spoons to mix. The bacon fat and butter may set when they hit the cold pumpkin, but they will quickly melt in the heat of the oven.

Spread the mixture in a shallow baking dish or microwave dish. Cover with foil or microwave film. Bake until the plums and pumpkin are tender, 50-60 minutes in the oven or 10-12 minutes in the microwave on high. Serve hot; great for a chilly evening!

RECAP

1 PREHEAT OVEN TO 190°C/375°F/GAS 5, ALLOWING 5 MINUTES FOR THIS BEFORE YOU START.

2 DICE BACON. MELT 15 G / ½ OZ BUTTER IN FRYING PAN AND FRY BACON UNTIL LIGHTLY BROWNED, 5-7 MINUTES. ADD REMAINING BUTTER TO PAN, TURN HEAT TO LOW AND LEAVE BUTTER TO MELT IN FAT.

3 MEANWHILE, HALVE PLUMS, DISCARDING STONES, AND PUT IN A LARGE BOWL. DISCARD SEEDS AND FIBRES FROM PUMPKIN. CUT SKIN AWAY FROM FLESH AND CUT FLESH INTO 2.5 CM / 1 IN CUBES. ADD TO PLUMS.

4 STIR SUGAR, CINNAMON, ALLSPICE, SALT AND PEPPER INTO BACON AND BUTTER. POUR OVER PLUMS AND PUMPKIN AND MIX WELL.

5 SPREAD MIXTURE IN SHALLOW BAKING DISH OR MICROWAVE DISH AND COVER WITH FOIL OR MICROWAVE FILM. BAKE UNTIL PLUMS AND PUMPKIN ARE TENDER, 50-60 MINUTES IN OVEN OR 10-12 MINUTES IN MICROWAVE ON HIGH. SERVE VERY HOT.

QUICK RATATOUILLE

TIME IN KITCHEN
12 minutes
STEWING *8-10 minutes*
STORAGE *up to 2 days in*
the refrigerator

serves 4

1 onion
4 tablespoons olive oil
1 medium aubergine
(about 375 g / ¾ lb)
2 garlic cloves
1 tablespoon ground
coriander
1 teaspoon dried
Provençal herbs or
dried thyme
1 red pepper
1 green pepper
500 g / 1 lb plum
tomatoes
2 small courgettes
(about 375 g / ¾ lb)
small bunch of basil
salt and freshly ground
black pepper

wok and stirrer

It was Elizabeth David, with her unmatched insight into French regional cooking, who first gave me the key to good ratatouille — a heaped spoonful of ground coriander. It's a spice that marries vegetables, oil and garlic — adding depth of flavour without being overwhelming. The wok is my idea — it not only speeds cooking, but ensures that the ratatouille does not overcook, which is important nowadays when everyone prefers their vegetables lightly done.

Ratatouille is a dish to make in summer when the four main ingredients — aubergines, peppers, courgettes and tomatoes (all of them vine fruit) — are at their best. Serve this ratatouille hot, chilled or at room temperature — the choice is yours. It's a dish which is good on its own as a light main course, or as a delicious accompaniment to grilled fish or chicken. If you have any left over, try the baked egg version below.

As always when using a wok, we'll add the more slowly cooked vegetables first. Peel the onion, leaving a little of the root. Cut it in half from the stem to root, set it cut side down on the board and thinly slice it. Heat the wok for 10 seconds, drizzle about 2 tablespoons of the oil around the sides and heat until almost smoking. Add the onion and leave to fry over a medium heat.

Trim the ends of the aubergine without peeling, and cut it in half lengthwise. Set the halves cut side down on the board and cut them lengthwise again into 3 or 4 strips. Finally cut these across into 1 cm / ⅜ in slices, forming generous chunks of aubergine. Stir the aubergine into the onion with the remaining oil and enough salt and pepper to flavour all the vegetables. Leave them to continue cooking.

Next, prepare the garlic — if it is added too soon it tends to scorch. Lightly crush the garlic cloves with the flat of the knife to loosen the skin and discard it. Smash them with the knife, then chop with the blade and stir into the vegetables with the coriander and Provençal herbs or thyme.

Halve the peppers, snap out the cores with your hands and discard the seeds. Put the halves cut side down on the cutting board and cut them across into thin slices. Stir them into the other vegetables.

Plum tomatoes have thin skins, so I don't bother to peel them. To chop them quickly: halve them across, squeeze out the seeds, place them cut side down on the cutting board and cut across first one way and then the next into 4 chunks. Stir them into the other vegetables. By now 6-8 minutes will have gone by and the vegetables should be starting to soften and brown lightly.

Finally, prepare the courgettes: trim the ends and halve the courgettes lengthwise. Set two side by side and cut them into 1 cm / ⅜ in slices. Stir them into the other vegetables, taste and adjust the seasoning.

Cover the wok and adjust the heat — the vegetables should cook fairly quickly but must not scorch. Leave the ratatouille to cook for 8-10 minutes. At this stage, all the vegetables will be soft, but they will still hold their shape. If you prefer them softer, in traditional style, leave them a little longer.

While they cook, pull the basil leaves from the stems and coarsely shred the leaves.

When the ratatouille is done to your taste, stir in the basil. You can serve the ratatouille hot or leave it to cool to room temperature (at least 30 minutes). If you can leave it longer, even up to 2 days, the flavour will mellow. Taste it once more and adjust the seasoning just before serving.

BAKED EGGS WITH RATATOUILLE

This recipe is a version of eggs 'au plat', a snack offered by innumerable French cafés as it can be cooked in a portable oven. The recipe is ideal for leftover ratatouille, so I've drafted it for only two people. Traditionally, eggs 'au plat' are cooked in shallow individual gratin dishes, but ramekins can be used too, when the eggs become 'en cocotte'. If you use ramekins, put only one egg in each and allow two of them per person – you'll have to increase cooking time by about 5 minutes.

Preheat the oven to 190°C/375°F/gas5, allowing 5 minutes for this before you start the recipe. Butter two individual gratin dishes. You'll need 1-2 cups of ratatouille. Reheat it in a frying pan, stirring so it warms evenly, and spread it in the dishes, making two hollows in the centre of each dish.

Sprinkle the hollows lightly with salt and pepper to season the eggs which are dropped into them. If topped with seasoning, the eggs will be spotty. Break 4 eggs, letting them fall into the hollows.

Bake them in the preheated oven for 8-12 minutes, until the egg whites are set but the yolks are still soft. Serve them at once.

RECAP

1 PEEL AND THINLY SLICE ONION. HEAT HALF OIL IN WOK, STIR IN ONION AND LEAVE TO FRY OVER MEDIUM HEAT.

2 TRIM AUBERGINE AND CUT IN HALF LENGTHWISE. CUT EACH HALF IN 3-4 STRIPS, THEN ACROSS INTO 1 CM / 3/8 IN SLICES. STIR INTO ONION WITH REMAINING OIL AND PLENTY OF SALT AND PEPPER. LEAVE TO COOK.

3 PEEL AND CHOP GARLIC. STIR INTO AUBERGINE WITH CORIANDER AND PROVENÇAL HERBS OR THYME.

4 HALVE, CORE AND SEED PEPPERS. CUT THEM ACROSS INTO THIN SLICES. STIR INTO VEGETABLES.

5 HALVE TOMATOES, SQUEEZE OUT SEEDS, THEN CHOP EACH HALF INTO 4 CHUNKS. STIR INTO OTHER VEGETABLES.

6 FINALLY TRIM COURGETTES, HALVE LENGTHWISE, THEN SLICE THEM ACROSS. STIR INTO OTHER VEGETABLES AND ADJUST SEASONING.

7 COVER WOK AND LEAVE TO COOK 8-10 MINUTES UNTIL ALL VEGETABLES ARE TENDER BUT STILL HOLD SHAPE.

8 MEANWHILE PULL BASIL LEAVES FROM STEMS AND COARSELY SHRED.

9 WHEN RATATOUILLE IS COOKED, STIR IN BASIL. SERVE HOT, OR LEAVE AT LEAST 30 MINUTES TO COOL TO ROOM TEMPERATURE. ADJUST SEASONING JUST BEFORE SERVING.

BLUE CHEESE PUFF

TIME IN KITCHEN
11 minutes
BAKING *30-40 minutes*

serves 4

You can personalize this recipe by using your local blue cheese, be it moist or firm, Danish, Stilton or Gorgonzola — it really doesn't matter. You're even free to use either Parmesan for a lighter puff or Gruyère, which gives a denser, richer result. In fact, I had trouble finding a title for the dish, as what results is a giant puff — a cross between a cheese choux pastry and a soufflé. Great fun and so simple. You can bake it in one large dish, as here, or in individual ramekins, which is quicker (15-20 minutes). Serve with a salad of bitter greens and, if you are adventurous, a glass of sweet white wine from late-picked grapes.

250 ml / 8 fl oz milk
45 g / 1½ oz butter,
 plus more for the
 dish
30 g / 1 oz flour
100 g / 3¼ oz grated
 Parmesan or Gruyère
 cheese
125 g / 4 oz blue cheese
3 eggs
freshly ground black
 pepper

2 litre / 3¼ pt shallow
soufflé dish or deep
baking dish

Preheat the oven to 190°C/375°F/gas5, allowing 5 minutes for this before you start.

Bring the milk to the boil with 30 g / 1 oz of the butter in a medium saucepan. Meanwhile, melt a little butter in a saucepan or use the microwave. Generously butter the soufflé or baking dish — one way to ensure a thick layer is to brush the dish with melted butter, chill it in the freezer for 10 minutes and then brush again.

Mix the flour, Parmesan or Gruyère cheese and pepper in a bowl, reserving a tablespoon of the cheese. When the milk boils and the butter is melted, take the pan from the heat and immediately tip in the flour mixture, stirring vigorously with a whisk until the mixture is smooth and thick.

Crumble the blue cheese into the flour mixture or cut it into dice with a knife and add the dice. Whisk until mixed, then return the pan to the heat and cook, whisking constantly, just until the blue cheese melts. Take the pan from the heat immediately as certain cheeses, such as Gruyère, cook into strings if left too long.

Add the eggs one by one, whisking to mix after each. I always taste the batter for seasoning at this point, but if you are concerned about eating raw eggs, there's no need to do so. Pour the batter into the buttered baking dish. Dot the top with the remaining butter and sprinkle with the reserved Parmesan or Gruyère.

Bake the batter in the preheated oven for 30-40 minutes until puffed and brown. The edges should be crisp and the centre slightly soft, like a Yorkshire pudding.

Set the dish on a plate lined with a napkin so it does not slip and take it at once to the table. Like a soufflé, it will shrink as soon as it starts to cool.

RECAP

1 PREHEAT OVEN TO 190°C/375°F/GAS5, ALLOWING 5 MINUTES FOR THIS BEFORE YOU START.

2 BRING MILK WITH 30 G / 1 OZ BUTTER TO BOIL IN MEDIUM PAN. MEANWHILE, GENEROUSLY BUTTER SOUFFLÉ OR BAKING DISH.

3 MIX FLOUR, PARMESAN OR GRUYERE AND PEPPER IN A BOWL, RESERVING A TABLESPOON OF CHEESE.

4 WHEN MILK BOILS AND BUTTER IS MELTED, TAKE PAN FROM HEAT, ADD FLOUR MIXTURE AND WHISK VIGOROUSLY UNTIL SMOOTH AND THICK.

5 CRUMBLE BLUE CHEESE INTO FLOUR MIXTURE AND WHISK UNTIL MIXED. RETURN PAN TO HEAT AND COOK, WHISKING CONSTANTLY, UNTIL BLUE CHEESE MELTS.

6 TAKE FROM HEAT AND WHISK IN EGGS ONE BY ONE. TASTE AND ADJUST SEASONING. SPREAD IN BUTTERED DISH. DOT TOP WITH REMAINING BUTTER AND SPRINKLE WITH RESERVED CHEESE.

7 BAKE 30-40 MINUTES UNTIL PUFFED AND BROWN. SERVE AT ONCE.

GRATED POTATO
& CHEESE GRATIN

TIME IN KITCHEN
7 minutes
BAKING 40-50 minutes
(14-18 in the
microwave)

serves 4-6

30 g / 1 oz butter
**150 ml / 5 fl oz double
cream**
**125 g / 4 oz cream
cheese**
3 eggs
**5-6 sprigs of rosemary,
sage or thyme**
**125 g / 4 oz grated
Gruyère cheese**
**2 tablespoons marc or
Cognac (optional)**
**½ teaspoon freshly
grated nutmeg**
**750 g / 1½ lb baking
potatoes**
salt and pepper

*food processor with
coarse grating blade
2 litre / 3¼ pt shallow
baking dish*

So many good vegetable dishes were developed in rural France for souper — the evening meal which normally starts with a good soup, hence our word 'supper'.

This gratin is best made with a floury baking potato which is grated in the processor, then mixed with grated cheese, cream cheese, eggs and cream. The batter bakes to a deliciously crisp cake with a soft centre, and begs for additions such as slivers of ham or cooked chicken, chunks of walnut or toasted hazelnut. I think of it as a winter dish, good with a salad of dandelion or escarole.

This recipe comes from the Morvan, the wild range of hills in central Burgundy. There they fortify the batter with a couple of tablespoons of marc or Cognac. Try it!

Preheat the oven to 200°C/400°F/gas6, allowing 5-10 minutes for this before you start the recipe. Spread the butter in the baking dish or a microwave dish.

The potatoes discolour very quickly when they are grated, so we'll mix all the other ingredients first. In a large bowl, whisk the cream into the cream cheese until soft — it is marginally quicker to do this with a hand-held electric mixer, but not much. Add the eggs and whisk again for about 1 minute until the batter is smooth.

Pull the herb leaves from the stems and chop them with a large knife — you can leave all but the rosemary in quite large pieces. Stir the chopped herbs into the batter, together with the grated cheese, marc or Cognac if using, nutmeg, salt and pepper, remembering that the potatoes will need generous amounts of seasoning.

Once again we don't have time to peel the potatoes, so simply rinse and dry them. Cut them into 2 or 3 pieces and push them down the feed tube of the processor fitted with the coarsest grating blade. If you don't have a processor, you can grate the potatoes on the coarsest grid of a box grater, but you'll need to allow a bit more time. Stir the grated potato into the cheese batter. I always taste and adjust seasoning at this stage, but if you are worried about raw eggs skip this step.

Spread the potato mixture in the buttered baking dish or microwave dish — it should form a layer about 2.5 cm / 1 in deep. Bake until crisp and golden brown on top, about 40-50 minutes in the preheated oven or 14-18 minutes in the microwave on high. Don't hesitate to keep cooking as the gratin is best very crisp, if anything slightly overdone. (After cooking in the microwave, brown the gratin for 1-2 minutes under the grill.)

Serve the gratin hot straight from the baking dish, cutting it into wedges.

RECAP

1 PREHEAT OVEN TO 200°C/400°F/GAS6, ALLOWING 5-10 MINUTES FOR THIS. SPREAD BUTTER IN BAKING OR MICROWAVE DISH.

2 IN LARGE BOWL, WHISK CREAM INTO CREAM CHEESE UNTIL SOFT, THEN WHISK IN EGGS. PULL HERB LEAVES FROM STEMS AND CHOP.

3 STIR HERBS, GRATED CHEESE, MARC OR COGNAC IF USING, NUTMEG, SALT AND PEPPER INTO BATTER.

3 RINSE AND DRY POTATOES. GRATE IN PROCESSOR, USING COARSEST BLADE OR USE BOX GRATER. STIR INTO CHEESE BATTER AND ADJUST SEASONING.

4 POUR BATTER INTO BUTTERED DISH AND BAKE UNTIL GRATIN IS CRISP AND VERY BROWN, 40-50 MINUTES IN OVEN OR 14-18 MINUTES IN MICROWAVE ON HIGH (THEN BROWN UNDER GRILL). SERVE HOT FROM BAKING DISH.

BAKED EGGS WITH ONIONS & CROUTONS

TIME IN KITCHEN
12 minutes
BAKING *12-15 minutes*
   (3½ in the microwave)

*serves 8 as a first course
   or 4 as a main course*

125 g / 4 oz butter
4 spring onions
4 slices of white bread
8 eggs
**125 ml / 4 fl oz double
   cream**
**salt and freshly ground
   black pepper**

*8 (150 ml / 5 fl oz)
   ramekins*

Odd how fashions in food come and go. Soufflés and omelettes have withstood the anti-egg crusade but scarcely anyone nowadays cooks an egg 'en cocotte', baking it in a ramekin topped with a spoonful of cream. The flavourings — be they a few cooked prawns or some sautéed mushrooms, or the spring onions and croûtes I suggest here — are put in the bottom of the dish and the egg takes only a few minutes to bake. Simplicity itself and a showcase for farm eggs if you can get them. In the microwave they cook perfectly and more quickly than a soft-boiled egg! Serve them with strips of toast.

Preheat the oven to 190°C/375°F/gas5. Put a folded tea towel in the bottom of a large roasting pan and add a generous layer of water to form a water bath. Bring the water to the boil over a high heat. You will need to allow 5-10 minutes for this before you start the recipe.

Melt 30 g / 1 oz of the butter in a frying pan over a low heat. Meanwhile, trim off the roots and part of the green tops of the spring onions and cut the stalks into thin diagonal slices. Stir them into the butter with salt and pepper and leave over a low heat for 4-5 minutes until soft and lightly browned.

Make the croûtons: melt the remaining butter over a low heat in a large frying pan. Trim off and discard the crusts from the bread, cut it into 1 cm / ⅜ in strips, then cut these across into cubes. Have ready a slotted spoon and a plate lined with paper towels. When the butter stops foaming, showing the whey has evaporated, stir in the bread cubes. Cook, stirring constantly, until they are evenly browned croûtons. They will colour quite quickly, so stir rapidly and lift the pan from the heat if they start browning too fast. Scoop them on to the paper towels to drain.

By now the spring onions should be soft. Spoon them into the ramekins and spread the croûtons on top. Sprinkle quite generously with salt and pepper, so the egg is seasoned as well. Break an egg into each ramekin and top with a tablespoon of cream. The cream shields the egg from the oven heat so that it sets without forming a crust. Don't be tempted to sprinkle with more seasoning as pepper will show as dark spots and salt causes pock marks on the eggs.

Gently lower the ramekins into the water bath. The cloth on the bottom of the pan shields the egg from direct heat and helps prevent water from bubbling into the egg. Bring the water back to the boil and transfer the bath to the oven. Cook the eggs for 12-15 minutes, depending on the thickness of the dishes, until the whites are almost set. The eggs will continue cooking for a minute or two in the heat of the dish and, when served, the egg whites should be just set and the yolks should still be soft.

If using the microwave, prick each egg yolk with the point of a knife so it does not burst during cooking. Set the ramekins on the microwave turntable and cook the eggs for 3½ minutes on high. They do not need a water bath.

Transfer the ramekins to 4 individual plates — tongs help with this if they are in a water bath. No garnish is added because the flavouring should be a surprise. The eggs are eaten with a teaspoon.

1 PREHEAT OVEN TO 190°C/375°F/GAS5. PUT FOLDED TEA TOWEL IN BOTTOM OF ROASTING PAN, ADD WATER AND BRING TO BOIL OVER HIGH HEAT. ALLOW 5-10 MINUTES FOR THIS BEFORE YOU START.

2 MELT 30 G / I OZ BUTTER IN FRYING PAN. MEANWHILE TRIM SPRING ONIONS AND THINLY SLICE. STIR INTO BUTTER WITH SALT AND PEPPER AND COOK OVER LOW HEAT 4-5 MINUTES UNTIL SOFT AND LIGHTLY BROWNED.

3 MAKE CROUTONS: MELT REMAINING BUTTER IN LARGE FRYING PAN. CUT BREAD INTO CUBES, DISCARDING CRUSTS. STIR CUBES INTO BUTTER AND FRY OVER MEDIUM HEAT, STIRRING CONSTANTLY SO THEY BROWN EVENLY. DRAIN ON PAPER TOWELS.

4 SPOON SPRING ONIONS INTO RAMEKINS AND SPREAD CROUTONS ON TOP. SEASON GENEROUSLY. BREAK AN EGG INTO EACH RAMEKIN AND TOP WITH TABLESPOON OF CREAM.

5 SET RAMEKINS IN WATER BATH AND BRING JUST BACK TO BOIL. COOK IN OVEN 12-15 MINUTES UNTIL WHITES OF EGGS ARE ALMOST SET. TRANSFER TO SERVING PLATES, ALLOWING 2 EGGS PER PERSON.

* IF USING MICROWAVE, NO NEED FOR WATER BATH. PRICK EGG YOLKS WITH POINT OF KNIFE. COOK 3½ MINUTES ON HIGH AND SERVE.

PLUM TOMATO & OREGANO FRITTATA

TIME IN KITCHEN
13 minutes
FRYING *25-35 minutes*

serves 4

The Italian 'frittata' is often translated as 'omelette', but it is actually rather different. Both are cooked on the hob, but an omelette is fried fast so it has a brown outside and soft centre, whereas a frittata is cooked as slowly as possible. The eggs gently puff and set to a golden cake that is cut in wedges and served hot or cold. A frittata can be flavoured with an assortment of vegetables and cheeses, even with meat or fish.

The frittata could have been specifically designed for our life in Burgundy. The gardener's wife, Madame Milbert, keeps hens and a few ducks, so fresh eggs are guaranteed. In summer, each month brings its harvest from the garden, starting with green peas and beans, then expanding to artichokes, spinach, courgettes and broccoli. At last the tomatoes come in, the filling for the very best frittata of all — flavoured with our own oregano and garlic. Stupendo! No accompaniment is needed, but a loaf of Italian-style country bread.

For frittata, the filling is cooked first, then the pan is wiped out before adding the eggs and filling. The correct frying pan size is important as the frittata will dry out if it is too large; while, if it is too small, the egg tends to scorch on the bottom before the top is cooked. Everyone has their favourite pan for cooking omelettes or frittata — I incline to the classic sloping-sided French steel pan. A heavy base is important to spread the heat evenly and a non-stick surface can be helpful.

2 tablespoons olive oil
1 onion
2 garlic cloves
500 g / 1 lb plum
    tomatoes
large bunch of fresh
    oregano
7 eggs
45 g / 1½ oz grated
    Gruyère cheese
30 g / 1 oz butter
salt and freshly ground
    black pepper

25-30 cm / 10-12 in
frying pan

Put the olive oil in the omelette pan over a steady low heat — note that cooking time for the frittata will vary with the size of the burner. Peel the onion, leaving a little of the root and cut it in half through root and stem. Set the halves cut side down on a board and thinly slice. Add the onion to the oil and leave to sauté over medium heat.

With the flat of the knife, lightly crush the garlic cloves to loosen and discard the skin. Smash the cloves with the flat of the knife, then chop them. Stir the garlic into the onion. We want it to cook lightly but not brown.

With the tip of the knife, scoop out the cores of the plum tomatoes, halve them across and squeeze out the seeds. Slice them with a large knife, then cut the slices across into quite small dice. Stir them into the onion mixture, sprinkle with salt and pepper and cook 1-2 minutes, just to soften them slightly without releasing too much juice. We don't have time to peel the tomatoes, so they will have a slightly chewy texture in the finished frittata.

Meanwhile, strip the oregano leaves from the stems, running your fingers along the stem from the tip to the root end, reserving a few sprigs for decoration.

Break the eggs into a bowl, add salt and pepper and whisk just until smooth and slightly frothy. With a spoon, stir in the tomato mixture from the pan (never mind that it is hot) together with the Gruyère and the oregano.

Wipe out the frying pan, replace it on the heat and add the butter. If you neglect this step and add the eggs directly to the vegetables, the frittata will stick. Heat the butter until foaming, then pour in the frittata mixture. Cover the pan with a lid and leave to cook over a low heat for 25-35 minutes. The frittata will puff and rise almost to the top of the pan. It is done when set on the top and well browned underneath when you lift the edge with a fork.

Run a knife around the edge of the frittata to loosen it and turn it out browned side up on a large warmed plate. Decorate the top with oregano sprigs. It is equally good at room temperature, when it shrinks and becomes more intense in flavour.

Frittata with Spinach & Goats' Cheese

I've substituted fresh goats' cheese for the ricotta that Italians would naturally use.

In the recipe above, omit the onions, plum tomatoes and oregano. Discard the stems from 500 g / 1 lb fresh spinach and wash and dry the leaves if they are not already washed.

Heat the oil in the frying pan and add the spinach. Cover the pan and cook over a medium heat for 1-2 minutes until the spinach is wilted. Meanwhile, peel and chop the garlic. Remove the lid, stir in the garlic with some salt, pepper and ground nutmeg. Continue cooking the spinach uncovered, stirring occasionally, for 3-5 minutes until all moisture has evaporated.

While the spinach is cooking, whisk the eggs with salt and pepper and crumble in 250 g / 8 oz fresh goats' cheese. When the spinach is cooked, spread it on a board to cool it slightly, then coarsely chop it and stir into the eggs. Melt the butter and cook the frittata as described.

RECAP

1 HEAT OIL IN OMELETTE PAN. PEEL AND SLICE ONION, ADD TO OIL AND LEAVE TO SAUTÉ. PEEL AND CHOP GARLIC AND STIR INTO ONION.

2 CORE TOMATOES, HALVE AND SQUEEZE OUT SEEDS. CHOP TOMATOES, STIR INTO ONION WITH SALT AND PEPPER AND LEAVE TO SAUTÉ 1-2 MINUTES.

3 MEANWHILE, STRIP OREGANO LEAVES FROM STEMS, KEEPING FEW SPRIGS FOR DECORATION.

4 WHISK EGGS WITH SALT AND PEPPER IN LARGE BOWL JUST UNTIL MIXED. STIR IN MIXTURE FROM PAN WITH GRUYERE AND OREGANO.

5 WIPE OUT FRYING PAN AND REPLACE ON HEAT.

MELT BUTTER UNTIL FOAMING. POUR IN MIXTURE, COVER PAN AND COOK OVER VERY LOW HEAT 25-35 MINUTES UNTIL SET ON TOP AND BROWNED UNDERNEATH.

6 TURN OUT ON LARGE WARMED PLATE AND DECORATE WITH OREGANO. SERVE HOT OR AT ROOM TEMPERATURE.

ROAST ROOT VEGETABLES WITH WALNUTS

TIME IN KITCHEN
   10 minutes
ROASTING *45-55 minutes*
   (20-22 in microwave)
serves 4

4 medium carrots
   (about 250 g / ½ lb)
2 turnips or
   ½ head of celeriac
   (about 250 g / ½ lb)
about 250 g / ½ lb baby
   beetroots
3 medium potatoes
   (about 500 g / 1 lb)
125 ml / 4 fl oz walnut
   oil or vegetable oil
8 shallots
8 garlic cloves
2 teaspoons sugar
1 teaspoon nutmeg
½ teaspoon allspice
60 g / 2 oz walnut
   pieces
1 teaspoon salt
½ teaspoon pepper

22.5 x 32.5 cm / 9 x 13 in
flameproof roasting pan

The current fashion for healthy vegetables cooked still with their skins is a boon for the busy cook. For this recipe I simply trim the vegetables, give them a scrub and then cut them into pieces so the cut sides absorb the flavours of the oil and spices. A light sprinkling of sugar also helps develop their inherent sweetness. Roast vegetables make wonderful accompaniments to any grilled or roast meats — just try them with venison!

Preheat the oven to 200°C/400°F/gas6. Allow 5-10 minutes for this before you start. Trim the carrots, turnips or celeriac and the beetroots, leaving a little of the green tops.

   Put the trimmed vegetables with the potatoes in a sink full of cold water and scrub them clean with a pot scrubber. Lift them out and dry on a tea towel. If you can only find cooked baby beetroots, that's fine — they need not be washed.

   Pour the oil into a large flameproof roasting pan and set over medium heat. As you cut the vegetables, add them directly to the heated oil so they start to cook at once. Quarter carrots and turnips lengthwise. If using celeriac, cut it into 4 wedges and cut each wedge in half. Halve the beets and cut potatoes into 2 or 3 pieces, scooping out any eyes. These careful directions are not just for appearance: the key to roasting vegetables is that they should all finish cooking at the same time. Therefore, roots that cook quickly — like potatoes — should be cut into larger pieces than carrots, which take longer. In general, turnips, celeriac and beets take about the same time, somewhere between potatoes and carrots. Add the shallots and garlic, both with their skins.

   Mix the sugar, nutmeg, allspice, walnuts, salt and pepper in a small bowl. Sprinkle over the vegetables and toss with two spoons until well coated with oil and flavourings.

   Cover the roasting pan with foil and roast until the vegetables are tender and browned, 45-55 minutes. If you stir them occasionally they will colour more evenly.

   If using the microwave, brown the vegetables well on the hob, then transfer them with the oil and flavourings to a microwave dish and cover with microwave film. Cook for 8 minutes on high. Stir thoroughly, cover and cook for 8 minutes longer. Stir again and cook, uncovered, 4-6 minutes longer, until all the vegetables are tender.

   The vegetables can be kept hot for a while, but lose their savour if reheated.

RECAP

1 PREHEAT OVEN TO 200°C/400°F/GAS6. TRIM VEGETABLES EXCEPT SHALLOTS AND GARLIC, LEAVING A LITTLE OF ANY GREEN TOPS. SCRUB CLEAN IN COLD WATER, DRY WELL.

2 PUT ROASTING PAN WITH OIL OVER MEDIUM HEAT, ADDING VEGETABLES AS YOU CUT THEM. QUARTER CARROTS AND TURNIPS, CUT CELERIAC INTO 4 WEDGES AND HALVE EACH WEDGE.

HALVE BEETROOTS AND CUT POTATOES INTO 2-3 PIECES. ADD SHALLOTS AND GARLIC IN SKINS.

3 MIX SUGAR, NUTMEG, ALLSPICE, WALNUTS, SALT AND PEPPER IN A SMALL BOWL. SPRINKLE OVER VEGETABLES AND MIX WELL.

4 COVER WITH FOIL AND ROAST UNTIL VEGETABLES ARE TENDER AND BROWNED, 45-55 MINUTES. IF TIME, STIR OCCASIONALLY.

* IF USING MICROWAVE, BROWN VEGETABLES WELL ON HOB. TRANSFER VEGETABLES AND FLAVOURINGS TO MICROWAVE DISH AND COVER WITH FILM. COOK 8 MINUTES ON HIGH, STIR AND COOK ANOTHER 8 MINUTES. STIR AGAIN AND COOK UNCOVERED 4-6 MINUTES UNTIL TENDER.

LENTILS WITH CORIANDER & BACON

TIME IN KITCHEN
  13 minutes
SIMMERING *1-1½ hours*
STORAGE *up to 2 days in
  the refrigerator*

serves 4

**150 g / 5 oz piece of
  lean bacon**
**2 tablespoons vegetable
  oil**
2 onions
4 carrots
500 g / 1 lb lentils
3 bay leaves
**1 tablespoon salt, or
  more if needed**
**1 teaspoon freshly
  ground black
  pepper, or more if
  needed**
**20 g / ¼ oz coriander
  seeds**

I tend to think there's not much to be done with lentils, but I think you'll enjoy this casserole, which makes a simple main dish. After trying out various types of lentil, I've found big meaty brown ones to be the best. There's no need to soak the lentils before cooking but it is important to wash them.

This dish reheats well and is a wonderful accompaniment to game or pork, as well as standing on its own as a simple main course. If you have any leftovers, purée the lentils in the processor and thin the purée with a little water for soup. Making double quantity for eight people is easy, but will extend cooking times by 15 minutes or so.

Slice the bacon into strips, discarding any rind, and cut the strips across into dice. Heat the oil in a heavy casserole and sauté the bacon over medium heat.

Meanwhile, peel the onions, leaving a little of the root. Cut them in half from the stem to root, set them cut sides down on the board and thinly slice them. Stir them into the bacon and continue sautéing.

Trim the carrots and rinse them in cold water, but don't bother to peel them. Cut lengthwise into quarters, then across into rough dice. Stir into the bacon and onions.

Put the lentils in a colander and rinse them under cold water, stirring them with your hands so they are thoroughly washed. Stir them into the bacon and vegetables and add 1 litre / 1⅔ pt water, the bay leaves, salt and pepper. Cover and bring to the boil.

Meanwhile, wrap the coriander seeds loosely in a plastic bag or plastic film. Pound them with the base of a heavy pan until coarsely crushed and stir them into the lentils.

When the lentils are boiling, turn the heat to low and partly cover so the lentils cook very gently. Leave them to simmer until the water is absorbed, anywhere from 1-1½ hours depending on the type.

When the water is absorbed, stir and taste the lentils. They should be very tender, but if not add another cup of water and continue simmering for 10-15 minutes longer. Be sure to cook lentils very thoroughly as they are indigestible – famous for their wind-producing properties – if at all crunchy. They keep and reheat very well.

Just before serving, discard the bay leaves, taste the lentils and adjust the seasoning.

RECAP

1 DICE BACON AND SAUTÉ IN OIL IN HEAVY CASSEROLE. PEEL AND SLICE ONIONS, STIR INTO BACON AND CONTINUE SAUTÉING. PEEL AND DICE CARROTS, ADD TO PAN AND SAUTÉ.

2 PUT LENTILS IN COLANDER AND WASH THOROUGHLY UNDER COLD RUNNING WATER. ADD TO BACON AND VEGETABLES WITH 1 LITRE / 1⅔ PT WATER, BAY LEAVES, SALT AND PEPPER. COVER POT AND BRING TO BOIL.

3 MEANWHILE, WRAP CORIANDER SEEDS IN PLASTIC BAG OR FILM AND POUND WITH HEAVY PAN UNTIL COARSELY CRUSHED. STIR INTO LENTILS.

4 WHEN BOILING, TURN HEAT TO LOW AND LEAVE LENTILS TO SIMMER, PARTLY COVERED, FOR 1-1½ HOURS DEPENDING ON TYPE.

5 WHEN WATER IS ABSORBED, STIR AND TASTE TO SEE IF LENTILS ARE TENDER. IF NOT, ADD A LITTLE MORE WATER AND CONTINUE SIMMERING 10-15 MINUTES.

6 WHEN COOKED, DISCARD BAY LEAVES AND ADJUST SEASONING.

PROVENÇAL TRICOLOR

TIME IN KITCHEN
12 minutes
BAKING *30-40 minutes*
STORAGE *up to 2 days in the refrigerator*

serves 4

3 garlic cloves
generous bunch of
    mixed herbs, such as
    rosemary, thyme,
    basil, sage and
    oregano
125 ml / 4 fl oz olive
    oil, or more
1 medium aubergine
    (about 750 g / 1½ lb)
2 large tomatoes
    (about 750 g / 1½ lb)
2 medium courgettes
    (about 500 g / 1 lb)
salt and pepper
½ lemon

food processor
22.5 x 32.5 cm / 9 x 13 in
baking dish

The colours of this dish — the red of tomato, the purple of aubergine and the green of courgette and herbs — instantly evoke Provence. The vegetables are simply sliced, arranged overlapping in a dish and baked with garlic and olive oil. This approach suits other vegetables as well: for instance, you can add cored and quartered red or green peppers, thinly sliced sweet onions, even sliced pumpkin, summer or butternut squash so that on a warm evening the dish becomes almost a meal in itself. It is also the ideal accompaniment for roast lamb or quickly grilled lamb chops. In Provence the baking dish is of glazed earthenware to spread the heat evenly, but any heatproof dish will do, preferably rectangular so the vegetables are easy to arrange.

Preheat the oven to 190°C/375°F/gas5. Allow 5 minutes for this before you begin the recipe.

To loosen the skin of the garlic, crush each clove lightly with the flat of a large knife, then discard the skin. Strip the herb leaves from the stems. Put garlic, herbs and half of the olive oil in the food processor and pulse the machine for about 15-20 seconds to chop the herbs coarsely. Spread the mixture in the bottom of the baking dish.

Cut the aubergine into 1 cm / ⅜ in slices, discarding each end. Slice the tomatoes in the same way, cutting them across and discarding the end slices. Slice the courgettes a bit thinner and also discard the ends. You'll find that this slicing goes quickly as the vegetables are left unpeeled to add flavour. To season them quickly, spread them on the cutting board and sprinkle with salt and pepper.

Arrange the vegetables overlapping and almost upright in the dish — you'll find they soften and fall sideways as they cook. Add 2 slices of courgette to every one of aubergine and tomato. Drizzle the remaining olive oil on top.

Bake the vegetables in the preheated oven for 30-40 minutes, until they are tender and lightly browned. Check them from time to time and, if they seem dry, sprinkle them with more olive oil.

The vegetables can be served hot, but in summer I prefer them at room temperature, sprinkled with a little lemon juice just before serving.

RECAP

1 PREHEAT OVEN TO 190°C/375°F/GAS5. ALLOW 5 MINUTES FOR THIS BEFORE YOU BEGIN.

2 PEEL GARLIC AND STRIP HERB LEAVES FROM STEMS. PUT BOTH IN FOOD PROCESSOR WITH HALF THE OIL AND PULSE UNTIL COARSELY CHOPPED. SPREAD OVER BOTTOM OF BAKING DISH.

3 CUT AUBERGINE AND TOMATOES INTO 1 CM / ⅜ IN SLICES AND COURGETTES SLIGHTLY THINNER; DISCARD ENDS. SPREAD SLICES ON BOARD AND SPRINKLE WITH SALT AND PEPPER.

4 ARRANGE VEGETABLES OVERLAPPING AND ALMOST UPRIGHT IN DISH, ADDING 2 SLICES OF COURGETTE TO EVERY ONE OF AUBERGINE AND TOMATO. DRIZZLE REMAINING OIL ON TOP.

5 BAKE 30-40 MINUTES UNTIL VEGETABLES ARE TENDER AND BROWNED. IF THEY SEEM DRY DURING COOKING, SPRINKLE WITH MORE OLIVE OIL.

6 SERVE HOT OR AT ROOM TEMPERATURE, SPRINKLED WITH A LITTLE LEMON JUICE.

FAST FINISHES

Perhaps one reason that desserts give so much pleasure is that they are a luxury rather than a necessity. Over the years I've developed a handful of easy ideas, some scarcely more complicated than the traditional French ending to a meal – cheese and fruit. For instance, in no time at all you can macerate seasonal fruits in wine, caramel or honey, or poach pears in a syrup of spiced red wine. You can freeze White Wine Granita like magic to just the right texture of crystalline snow, thanks to its sugar and high alcohol content.

Moving a step further, whipping egg whites or cream in a mixer takes only 2-3 minutes, bringing within reach a simple Chocolate Mousse, or for that matter a Raspberry Fool of whipped cream layered with berries and grated chocolate. We can even prepare a cake in the allotted 15 minutes – Breton Butter Cake which calls for only four ingredients, all of them store-cupboard staples. For more festive occasions, a soufflé can be whipped up astonishingly fast. In summer you can turn to a cream-topped version of crème brûlée, layered with strawberries and topped with caramel – all can be prepared well within our 15-minute limit.

Don't even think about making conventional tarts and pies in 15 minutes, as the pastry takes far too long. Frozen filo pastry dough is another matter. With a discreet brushing of butter, it will bake to admirable flaky crispness. Here I suggest you use it to make a strudel with the traditional filling of cherries, cinnamon and brown sugar, and a novel Moroccan galette stuffed with dried fruit and chocolate.

If expecting guests, dessert is the first dish I think of preparing ahead. All the cold desserts keep happily, so you can easily make them the night before. The hot desserts are quick to prepare, but – with the exception of Strawberry Burnt Cream – they do take time to cook. So it's lucky they come at the end of the meal. After an opening glass of wine and a leisurely main course, even Plum Batter Pudding will be cooked to perfection!

left PEPPERED PEARS IN RED WINE *see page 106*

See back jacket

PEPPERED PEARS IN RED WINE

TIME IN KITCHEN
8 minutes
SIMMERING *30-40 minutes (10-12 in the microwave)*
STORAGE *up to 2 days in the refrigerator*

serves 4

4 large pears, with their stems (about 1 kg / 2 lb)
100 g / 3¼ oz sugar
1 bottle (750 ml / 1¼ pt) red wine
1 cinnamon stick
1 tablespoon black peppercorns
1 lemon

This recipe will fill your kitchen with the warm spicy smell of mulled wine. Don't waste a good vintage, but use one of those fruity wines that taste grapey in the glass — they make deliciously rich syrup for poaching.

Although any firm pear will do, this recipe is perfect for long-necked Conference pears as they hold their shape well during cooking. You can poach up to a dozen pears at a time — just increase the spiced syrup in proportion and be sure the pears are immersed as they cook. Here's an opportunity for the microwave to save you time.

On a chilly day I like to serve the pears warm with a slice of Breton Butter Cake (see page 121) or crisp ginger biscuits for dipping. In summer, chill the pears and set them in a chilled bowl on a bed of vanilla ice-cream, spooning the dark shiny syrup on top.

Put the sugar, wine, cinnamon stick and peppercorns in a small pan just big enough to hold the pears and deep enough for the syrup to cover them completely.

Bring the syrup slowly to the boil, stirring once or twice. Ensure that all the sugar dissolves before the syrup boils, or it may crystallize. Pare off the lemon zest and add to the syrup as it heats. If using the microwave, cook the syrup in a microwave bowl for 3 minutes on high.

Meanwhile, peel the pears leaving the stem and scoop out the flower end. The stem not only looks pretty, it is also useful as a handle for lifting the pear. To prevent the pears discolouring, immerse them at once in the wine mixture even if it is not yet boiling, arranging them upright if possible. Set a heavy heatproof plate on top of the pears so that they are completely covered in syrup or they will develop a white 'tide line'.

Bring the syrup just to the boil and poach very gently (the syrup should scarcely simmer) for 30-40 minutes, until the pears look translucent and are very tender when pierced with the point of a knife. Cooking time varies very much with the ripeness of the pears. Ensure they are thoroughly cooked or they will discolour around the core. Alternatively, put the pears in a microwave bowl, cover with film and cook for 10-12 minutes in the microwave on high, or until tender.

Transfer the pears to a bowl and if they do not sit upright, cut a thin slice from the base so they do. Make sure no peppercorns have stuck to them.

Stir the syrup, loosening any spices stuck to the base of the pan. Return the pan to the heat and boil uncovered for 7-10 minutes, reducing the syrup until it is dark and rich but not sticky (as so often, the best test is to taste it). Strain it over the pears.

SPICED FIGS IN RED WINE

Figs take kindly to the same mulled wine treatment as pears, but their cooking time is much, much shorter. I suggest adding sliced fresh root ginger instead of peppercorns. For a change of emphasis, fresh cream cheese or yogurt is a pleasant contrast as accompaniment.

Make the poaching syrup as described in the recipe above, substituting a walnut-sized piece of fresh ginger, cut in slices, for the peppercorns. In place of the pears, pack 12 purple or green figs in the hot syrup — they should all touch the base of the pan.

Bring the syrup to the boil and poach gently uncovered just until the figs are tender, 4-6 minutes.

Turn off the heat and transfer the figs to a plate, lifting them with their stems or using a draining spoon. Bring the syrup back to the boil and boil for 8-10 minutes, until glossy and slightly thick.

Meanwhile trim the stems of the figs and cut a deep cross in each one so the pink centre is exposed and arrange them in 4 individual shallow bowls. Strain the syrup into a jug and pour it over the figs. Serve them warm or chilled.

RECAP

1 PUT SUGAR, WINE, CINNAMON STICK AND PEPPERCORNS IN A SMALL DEEP PAN AND BRING SLOWLY TO BOIL. PARE LEMON ZEST AND ADD IT TO SYRUP AS IT HEATS.

2 MEANWHILE, PEEL PEARS, LEAVING STEMS AND SCOOPING OUT FLOWER ENDS. IMMEDIATELY

IMMERSE PEARS IN SYRUP, STANDING UPRIGHT IF POSSIBLE. SET A SMALL HEATPROOF PLATE ON TOP TO KEEP THEM COMPLETELY IMMERSED IN SYRUP.

3 BRING JUST TO A BOIL AND SIMMER 30-40 MINUTES, UNTIL PEARS ARE VERY TENDER WHEN PIERCED WITH A KNIFE.

* ALTERNATIVELY, PUT PEARS IN MICROWAVE BOWL, COVER WITH FILM AND COOK IN MICROWAVE 10-12 MINUTES ON HIGH, OR UNTIL TENDER.

4 TRANSFER PEARS TO A BOWL. BOIL SYRUP UNCOVERED FOR 7-10 MINUTES, UNTIL DARK AND RICH. STRAIN OVER PEARS.

CHERRY STRUDEL

TIME IN KITCHEN
11 minutes
BAKING *25-30 minutes*

serves 4

Authentic strudel pastry takes not only time but also much practice in pulling the elastic dough into a metre-square sheet so thin that you can read a newspaper through it. Ready-prepared filo dough may be less moist and tender, but it is crisper and infinitely quicker to use. You need merely minutes to brush the layers of dough with melted butter, sprinkle them with the classic filling of cherries, cinnamon, lemon and brown sugar, and then roll the strudel with the help of a cloth. This recipe assumes you use canned stoned cherries — bitter ones are best — but if you have time to stone some fresh ones, you'll be richly rewarded. For serving, a bowl of sour cream is just right, with the strudel warm or at room temperature.

**45 g / 1½ oz unsalted
   butter**
1 lemon
60 g / 2 oz brown sugar
**½ teaspoon ground
   cinnamon**
**375 g / 12 oz can of
   stoned bitter
   cherries**
**4 large sheets of
   filo dough
   (about 60 g / 2 oz)**
**icing sugar for
   sprinkling**

Preheat the oven to 190°C/375°F/gas5, allowing 5 minutes for this before you start.

Melt the butter in a small pan over a low heat or in the microwave. Finely grate the lemon zest. To make cleaning the grater easy, stretch a piece of plastic film over the grid and grate the lemon on top of it – the zest will be left on the film. Mix the zest with the brown sugar and cinnamon in a small bowl. Drain the cherries.

Take the butter from the heat. Have a damp tea towel ready as filo dough dries out very fast. Lay a dry tea towel on the work surface, short side nearest you. Unwrap the filo dough and transfer one sheet to the dry towel, also laying a short end nearest to you. Cover the remaining sheets of dough with the damp towel. Brush the sheet of dough with melted butter. Sprinkle with about one-quarter of the cherries and a quarter of the sugar mixture. Lay another sheet of dough on top, brush it with butter and add more filling. Repeat with two more layers of dough, using all the filling. Wrap leftover dough tightly and keep it for another use.

To make the filled layers easier to roll, fold the two corners of dough nearest you inwards about 2.5 cm / 1 in. Pull upwards on the edge of towel nearest to you so the dough starts to form a fairly tight roll. Keep rolling until all the filling is enclosed. Butter a baking sheet and transfer the roll to it, seam side down. Brush the top with butter.

Bake in the preheated oven for 25-30 minutes, until it is crisp and brown and a skewer inserted in the centre for 20 seconds is hot to your touch when withdrawn.

Leave the strudel to cool on the baking sheet for about 10 minutes. If you are serving it warm, sprinkle it generously with icing sugar and cut it at once in 4 diagonal slices using a serrated knife. Transfer the slices to plates – the trimmings are the perks of the cook! If serving the strudel cool, sprinkle it with sugar and slice it only just before serving so it stays moist. Pass a bowl of sour cream separately.

RECAP

1 PREHEAT OVEN TO 190°C/375°F/GAS5, ALLOWING 5 MINUTES FOR THIS BEFORE YOU START.

2 MELT BUTTER AND FINELY GRATE LEMON ZEST. MIX ZEST WITH SUGAR AND CINNAMON IN SMALL BOWL. DRAIN CHERRIES.

3 LAY DRY TEA TOWEL ON WORK SURFACE, SHORT SIDE NEAREST YOU. UNWRAP FILO DOUGH AND LAY A SHEET ON TOWEL. COVER REMAINING DOUGH WITH DAMP CLOTH SO IT DOES NOT DRY OUT. BRUSH SHEET WITH BUTTER AND SPRINKLE WITH ONE-QUARTER OF CHERRIES AND SUGAR MIXTURE. TOP WITH ANOTHER LAYER OF DOUGH, BUTTER IT AND ADD FILLING. CONTINUE UNTIL 4 SHEETS OF DOUGH AND ALL THE FILLING ARE USED.

4 FOLD DOUGH CORNERS NEAREST YOU INWARDS ABOUT 2.5 CM / 1 IN. PULL UPWARDS ON EDGE OF TOWEL NEAREST TO YOU SO DOUGH ROLLS INTO QUITE A TIGHT CYLINDER. BUTTER BAKING SHEET AND TRANSFER ROLL TO IT, SEAM SIDE DOWN. BRUSH ROLL WITH BUTTER.

5 BAKE 25-30 MINUTES UNTIL CRISP AND BROWN AND SKEWER INSERTED IN CENTRE FOR 20 SECONDS IS HOT TO TOUCH WHEN WITHDRAWN.

6 SERVE HOT OR AT ROOM TEMPERATURE. JUST BEFORE SERVING, SPRINKLE GENEROUSLY WITH ICING SUGAR AND CUT IN 4 DIAGONAL SLICES WITH SERRATED KNIFE, DISCARDING ENDS. SERVE BOWL OF SOUR CREAM SEPARATELY.

See page 6

PLUM BATTER PUDDING

TIME IN KITCHEN
8 minutes
BAKING 50-60 minutes
STANDING 5-10 minutes

serves 4

It's odd, really, that the Yorkshire pudding principle of a baked batter so rarely extends to dessert in England. The French version of batter pudding, called clafoutis, *originated in the Limousin in central France; but now you'll find it everywhere, adapted to local fruits and alcohols. Traditional* clafoutis *is made with small bitter cherries, but the season is so short that I'm suggesting plums or dried prunes. Apricots are another alternative. If you do use cherries, leave in the stones for flavour.*

The last-minute sprinkle of alcohol on the pudding should echo the fruit — slivovitz or white prune *(plum brandy) for plums and prunes, apricot liqueur for apricots and kirsch for cherries. You can abstain if there are children in the family, offering instead a bowl of plain yogurt, egg custard, or the French choice of crème fraîche.*

500 g / 1 lb plums or
   250 g / ½ lb stoned
   prunes
butter for the dish
60 g / 2 oz sugar, plus
   more for the dish
4 eggs
30 g / 1 oz flour
pinch of salt
250 ml / 8 fl oz milk
3 tablespoons slivovitz,
   prune or other
   alcohol (see above)
icing sugar for
   sprinkling

1.5 litre / 2⅓ pt shallow
   baking dish

Preheat the oven to 190°C/375°F/gas5, allowing 5 minutes for this before you start the recipe.

Butter the baking dish, sprinkle it with sugar and twist the dish so it is evenly coated, discarding excess sugar.

Rinse the plums under cold water in a colander. Cut them in half with a small knife, running it around the indentation in the fruit, then twisting each half to loosen them from the stone. Discard the stones and spread the plum halves in the baking dish. They should all touch the base of the dish. If using prunes, spread them also in the dish.

Make the batter: put the sugar in a bowl, break in the eggs and whisk for 1-2 minutes until light and frothy. Stir in the flour and salt just until smooth. Don't be tempted to beat the batter as this will develop the gluten in the flour and tend to make the pudding tough. Stir in the milk. Strain the batter over the plums or prunes — the strainer will remove any lumps of flour.

Bake the pudding in the preheated oven for 50-60 minutes until it is puffed and brown. It should be firm in the centre and will have started to pull away from the sides of the dish.

Let it cool for 5-10 minutes, then sprinkle with the alcohol. Dust it generously with icing sugar and serve warm.

R E C A P

1 PREHEAT OVEN TO 190°C/375°F/GAS5, ALLOWING 5 MINUTES FOR THIS BEFORE YOU START.

2 BUTTER BAKING DISH AND COAT WITH SUGAR. RINSE PLUMS AND HALVE, DISCARDING STONES. SPREAD THEM, OR PRUNES IF USING, IN BAKING DISH.

3 MAKE BATTER: WHISK EGGS AND SUGAR IN BOWL. ADD FLOUR AND SALT AND STIR JUST UNTIL MIXED. STIR IN MILK. STRAIN BATTER OVER FRUIT.

4 BAKE 50-60 MINUTES UNTIL PUFFED AND BROWN. LET COOL 5-10 MINUTES, THEN SPRINKLE WITH ALCOHOL. TOP GENEROUSLY WITH ICING SUGAR AND SERVE WARM.

ORANGE SALAD WITH CARAMEL

TIME IN KITCHEN
14 minutes
CHILLING *30 minutes,*
or up to 24 hours in
the refrigerator

serves 4

150 g / 5 oz sugar
vegetable oil for the
baking sheet
60 g / 2 oz pecan pieces
or walnut halves
4 large navel oranges

Few desserts are more refreshing than this simple salad. Look for large navel oranges — distinguished by the 'navel' mark of a baby orange at the top of the fruit — as they have no seeds and are perfect for slicing. This recipe is also spectacular made with brilliant blood oranges, though as they are smaller you'll need to allow two per person.

Here we're going to make a caramel with sugar syrup, both to sweeten the oranges and to add flavour. Half of the caramel is mixed with nuts and hardens so it can be crushed for a crisp topping, while the rest is dissolved in water for sauce.

You'll need a small pan with a heavy base for making caramel, so the heat is spread and the syrup browns evenly. Put the sugar with 125 ml / 4 fl oz of water in the pan and heat fairly gently until the sugar dissolves. Do not stir, but shake the pan from time to time to mix the sugar in with the water.

Meanwhile, generously oil a baking sheet and pile the nuts on it.

Prepare the oranges: with a serrated knife, cut a slice from the top and bottom of an orange, slicing through to the flesh. Set the fruit upright on the chopping board. Holding the knife almost horizontally and starting at the top, cut away rind, pith and skin, following the curve of the fruit so the flesh of the orange is uncovered. Continue cutting from top to bottom, working around the orange, until the flesh is completely free of pith and skin. Hold the orange sideways and cut across the segments into 6 mm / ¼ in slices, leaving them in a pile. Slide the knife under the pile and transfer the slices to an individual serving plate. Fan the slices out. Repeat with the remaining oranges.

While cutting the oranges, keep an eye on the syrup. As soon as the sugar has dissolved, turn up the heat and let it boil without stirring. This is important as if stirred it tends to crystallize. After 4-6 minutes bubbles will burst more slowly, showing most of the water has evaporated. A minute or two later the syrup will start to colour around the edges. Turn down the heat slightly and watch carefully as within 30-60 seconds it will cook to a deep golden caramel. If it is cooking unevenly, shake the pan gently.

When the caramel starts to smoke and is fairly dark, take it from the heat and pour about half the syrup over the nuts on the baking sheet. Not all of the nuts will be covered but this is fine as they will be crushed with the caramel later. Leave this nut caramel to cool and go crisp and hard.

Immediately make the sauce: add 4 tablespoons of water to the rest of the caramel in the pan, holding it well away from you as it will spatter. Do this quickly, as the caramel will continue to cook in the heat of the pan and will be bitter if it is too dark. Return to the heat and boil the caramel for 1-2 minutes so it dissolves in the water and thickens very slightly until syrupy. Set it aside while you finish the oranges, then spoon the sauce over them. Chill in the refrigerator for about 30 minutes.

When the nut caramel is hard (4 or 5 minutes), lift it off the baking sheet, loosening it with a metal spatula under it, if necessary. Put it in a sturdy plastic bag and pound it with a rolling pin, breaking it into small chips. Just before serving the oranges, sprinkle them with crispy nut caramel. You can make the salad up to a day ahead, but keep the crisp caramel tightly covered as it softens in humid air.

Orange Salad with Honey Caramel

Honey makes an aromatic caramel and takes a little longer to cook than sugar.

In the recipe above, omit the nuts. Substitute 150 g / 5 oz honey for the sugar and make a crisp honey caramel with half the syrup. Use the remaining syrup to make sauce as described.

RECAP

1 *PUT SUGAR WITH 125 ML / 4 FL OZ WATER IN SMALL HEAVY PAN AND HEAT UNTIL SUGAR DISSOLVES. GENEROUSLY OIL BAKING SHEET AND PILE NUT PIECES ON IT.*

2 *USING SERRATED KNIFE, PEEL ORANGES, CUTTING OFF SKIN AND PITH DOWN TO FLESH. CUT FLESH INTO 6 MM / ¼ IN SLICES AND ARRANGE OVERLAPPING ON 4 SERVING PLATES.*

3 *MEANWHILE, KEEP AN EYE ON SYRUP. WHEN SUGAR HAS DISSOLVED, BOIL SYRUP 4-6 MINUTES WITHOUT STIRRING UNTIL IT STARTS TO CARAMELIZE. LOWER HEAT SLIGHTLY AND CONTINUE COOKING TO DEEP GOLDEN CARAMEL. POUR ABOUT HALF CARAMEL OVER NUTS AND LEAVE TO SET.*

4 *ADD 4 TABLESPOONS WATER TO REMAINING CARAMEL, STANDING BACK AS IT WILL SPATTER. BOIL 1-2 MINUTES UNTIL DISSOLVED TO LIGHT SAUCE. SPOON SAUCE OVER THE ORANGE SLICES. CHILL AT LEAST 30 MINUTES.*

5 *WHEN NUT CARAMEL IS SET HARD, PUT IN PLASTIC BAG AND POUND TO SMALL CHIPS WITH A ROLLING PIN. JUST BEFORE SERVING, SPRINKLE EACH PLATE WITH PECAN CARAMEL.*

See page 5

MOROCCAN DRIED FRUIT & CHOCOLATE GALETTES

TIME IN KITCHEN
14 minutes
BAKING *20-25 minutes*
STORAGE *up to 8 hours
in an airtight
container*

serves 4

60 g / 2 oz unsalted
butter
60 g / 2 oz bittersweet
chocolate
75 g / 2½ oz walnut
pieces
30 g / 1 oz dried
apricots
30 g / 1 oz dried figs
1 packet of filo dough

Brik dough, the Moroccan version of Greek filo, is slightly thicker and more robust, almost like an Oriental rice wrapper made with wheat flour. It is used for the famous b'staela, a layered pastry pie filled with a scrumptious mix of pigeon, fresh coriander, saffron, cinnamon and sugar. Other fillings may be sweet with dried fruit and nuts, as in these galettes. Use blanched pistachios if they aren't too costly, though here I suggest less expensive walnut pieces. The filling is bound with chocolate, a lavish mixture disguised by the deceptively modest pastry case.

If you can find brik dough, by all means use it. Here I suggest frozen filo, which is available in most good grocery shops. I can't give you an exact weight as the sheets of dough vary in size, but 4 sheets of filo that measure about 30 cm / 12 in square will be about right. I leave you to play architect and trim them to size. For fun, you can loosely pleat trimmings of dough into giant roses to set atop the baked galettes.

Preheat the oven to 190°C/375°F/gas5, allowing 5 minutes for this before you start.

Melt the butter over a low heat in a small pan or warm it in the microwave. Using a large chef's knife, chop the chocolate – it should be fairly fine but still contain a few chunks to give texture. Put it in a bowl with the walnuts. Also chop the apricots and figs quite finely and add to the bowl – they will stick to the knife and you may find that it helps to rinse the blade under warm water. Stir to mix the filling.

Filo dough dries very quickly once opened, so have a damp tea towel ready or use paper towel. Unwrap the filo dough and unroll the sheets. Take one sheet of dough from the pile and set it on the work surface. Lightly brush the sheet with butter, lay another sheet on top of it and brush it also with butter. Continue until you have 4 layers. If the stack of filo starts to dry out while you are working, cover it with the damp cloth. You may have leftover filo for another recipe.

Butter the baking sheet. Cut four 15 cm / 6 in squares from the filo layers and reserve the trimmings for decoration. Spoon the filling evenly in the centre of each of the four squares.

To wrap each galette: pull in the corners of the square, overlapping them to cover the filling completely. Flip over the galette, flatten with the palm of your hand and cup your hands around it to make a neat round, as if shaping a hamburger.

Set the galettes on a baking sheet, seams underneath, and brush with butter. If you have time, loosely roll any pastry trimmings and twist the rolls into four spiral 'roses'. Set them on the baking sheet. Alternatively, you can simply cut four holes in the top of each galette to make it look like a button. The holes also act as vents for steam.

Bake the galettes in the preheated oven for 20-25 minutes until brown and crisp. A metal skewer inserted in the centre for 20 seconds should be hot to your touch when withdrawn. Roses will be crisp and lightly brown after 12-15 minutes, so remove them first. Transfer roses and galettes to a wire rack to cool.

Serve the galettes warm or cool, sprinkled with icing sugar and topped with a pastry rose if you have made them. When you open a galette you will find that the chocolate has melted to a luscious cream.

1 PREHEAT OVEN TO 190°C/375°F/GAS5, ALLOWING 5 MINUTES FOR THIS BEFORE YOU START.

2 MELT BUTTER. MEANWHILE, CHOP CHOCOLATE, APRICOTS AND FIGS WITH LARGE KNIFE. MIX IN BOWL WITH WALNUTS.

3 UNWRAP FILO AND LAY ONE SHEET ON WORK SURFACE. BRUSH LIGHTLY WITH MELTED BUTTER. ADD ANOTHER SHEET, BRUSHING IT WITH BUTTER. CONTINUE UNTIL YOU HAVE 4 LAYERS. BUTTER BAKING SHEET.

4 CUT FOUR 15 CM / 6 IN SQUARES FROM THE FILO. SPOON A QUARTER OF FILLING IN CENTRE OF EACH. TO SHAPE: PULL IN CORNERS OF SQUARE TO COVER FILLING COMPLETELY. FLIP GALETTE AND FLATTEN IT, SHAPING IN A ROUND LIKE A HAMBURGER. SET ON BAKING SHEET AND BRUSH WITH BUTTER.

5 IF TIME, LOOSELY ROLL DOUGH TRIMMINGS, TWIST INTO 4 ROSES AND SET ON BAKING SHEET. BAKE UNTIL CRISP AND BROWN, ALLOWING 12-15 MINUTES FOR ROSES AND 20-25 MINUTES FOR GALETTES.

6 TRANSFER PASTRIES TO RACK TO COOL. SPRINKLE WITH ICING SUGAR, TOPPING EACH WITH A PASTRY ROSE. THEY MAY BE SERVED WARM OR COOL.

HONEY-BAKED APPLES WITH CHOCOLATE

TIME IN KITCHEN
 8 minutes
BAKING *40-50 minutes*
STORAGE *up to 2 days in the refrigerator*
serves 4

4 medium apples
 (about 750 g / 1½ lb)
125 g / 4 oz dessert or semi-sweet chocolate
4 generous tablespoons honey
 (about 100 g / 3¼ oz)

This recipe evolved by accident, on an occasion when I ran out of raisins for stuffing a baked apple and, in desperation, used chocolate instead — with delicious results.

It is important to use a tart variety of apple that will be fluffy and juicy when baked; traditional favourites are Cox's or Reine des Reinettes, though you can always fall back on the ubiquitous Granny Smith. Baked apples are best straight from the oven — but watch out, the insides will be scalding hot!

Preheat the oven to 190°/375°F/gas 5 — allow 5 minutes for this before you begin.

Wipe the apples and cut out the core. If you don't have an apple corer, use a vegetable peeler, forcing it down through the centre of the apple then twisting to loosen the core. Repeat the action until you've scooped out a cavity with a diameter of about 2.5 cm / 1 in, large enough to fit the squares of chocolate. Slash the skin of each apple horizontally around its 'equator' so the flesh can expand without bursting the skin. Break the chocolate into squares and push some into the hollow of each apple.

Set the apples in a shallow baking dish; they should not quite touch each other in the dish so heat can circulate. Pour over 125 ml / 4 fl oz water and top each apple with a spoonful of honey.

Bake the apples in the preheated oven for 40-50 minutes, until they are tender when pierced with a skewer. If you have time, baste occasionally so the honey forms a glaze on the apples. Towards the end of cooking, keep an eye on the dish and add more water if the honey shows signs of scorching.

Serve the apples hot, with the honey syrup spooned over as a sauce.

HONEY-BAKED APPLES WITH CHOCOLATE

RECAP

1 PREHEAT OVEN TO 190°/375°F/GAS 5 — ALLOW 5 MINUTES FOR THIS BEFORE YOU BEGIN.

2 WIPE APPLES, CORE AND SLASH SKIN AROUND EQUATORS. STUFF WITH CHOCOLATE.

3 SET APPLES IN BAKING DISH, POUR OVER 125 ML / 4 FL OZ WATER AND TOP EACH APPLE WITH SPOONFUL OF HONEY.

4 BAKE FOR 40-50 MINUTES, UNTIL TENDER, ADDING MORE WATER IF NECESSARY. SERVE HOT WITH HONEY SYRUP SPOONED OVER AS A SAUCE.

MARMALADE SOUFFLÉ

TIME IN KITCHEN
12 minutes
BAKING *7-10 minutes*
STANDING *up to 2 hours*
in the refrigerator
before baking

serves 4

Were it not such fun, I would hesitate to suggest that this simple marmalade soufflé qualifies as a recipe at all. It consists of light meringue mixed with melted marmalade, of the finely cut or jelly type. Choose lemon, orange, lime — whatever flavour you prefer. If you happen to make your own marmalade, what better way to show it off? If not, look for a good commercial brand with no added sugar. For a party, don't hesitate to double the recipe, as most mixers can accommodate the whites of eight eggs.

The very first orange marmalade is said to have been made for Mary Queen of Scots, who was brought up at the French court. On her return to Edinburgh at the age of 18, she found Scotland chilly and harsh. One day when she was ailing, her French cook invented a new preserve to cheer her spirits and called it 'Marie est malade'. It's a pretty story, though sceptics counter that 'marmelade' was already the term used in France for fruit butters. To continue the Scottish theme, you might offer shortbread with the soufflé.

15-30 g / ½-1 oz butter
200 g / 6½ oz lemon
marmalade
whites of 4 eggs
pinch of salt
60 g / 2 oz caster sugar

4 large ramekins
(250 ml / 8 fl oz)
food mixer

Preheat the oven to 190°C/375°F/gas5, allowing 5 minutes for this before you start.

Melt the butter in a small pan or the microwave and brush the ramekins. Put the marmalade with 4 tablespoons of water to melt over a medium heat.

Meanwhile, put the egg whites in a mixer with a pinch of salt and start whisking at medium speed. The salt helps the whites break up and whisk to a smooth foam. As soon as the whites are frothy, increase the speed to maximum and whisk for 2-3 minutes, until very stiff. With the whisk turning, pour in the sugar and continue whisking for 30-60 seconds until the egg whites are glossy and have formed a light meringue. The whites will soften slightly and form quite long peaks when you lift the whisk.

Meanwhile, keep an eye on the marmalade. When it is melted and smooth, take it from the heat and set aside.

When the meringue is ready, add about one-quarter to the warm marmalade and stir together quite thoroughly. This light mixture is now much easier to fold into the remaining meringue. Add the mixture to the meringue and fold them both together as lightly as possible. Stop folding as soon as the mixture is smooth. Spoon it into the prepared ramekins, shaping a decorative shallow peak in the middle.

Set the ramekins on a baking sheet and bake the soufflés in the preheated oven for 7-10 minutes until puffed and brown — the peak will be quite dark.

Prepare 4 serving plates, set the ramekins on them and serve at once.

RECAP

1 PREHEAT OVEN TO 190°C/375°F/GAS5, ALLOWING 5 MINUTES FOR THIS BEFORE YOU START. BRUSH RAMEKINS WITH BUTTER.

2 MELT MARMALADE WITH 4 TABLESPOONS WATER.

3 MEANWHILE, STIFFLY WHISK EGG WHITES WITH PINCH OF SALT. ADD SUGAR AND CONTINUE WHISKING 30-60 SECONDS TO MAKE A LIGHT MERINGUE.

4 STIR ABOUT ONE-QUARTER OF MERINGUE INTO MELTED, STILL WARM MARMALADE. ADD THIS TO REMAINING MERINGUE AND FOLD TOGETHER.

5 SPOON MIXTURE INTO PREPARED RAMEKINS, MAKING SHALLOW PEAKS IN CENTRES. BAKE 7-10 MINUTES UNTIL PUFFED AND BROWN.

6 SET RAMEKINS ON INDIVIDUAL PLATES AND SERVE AT ONCE.

CHOCOLATE MOUSSE WITH ORANGE

TIME IN KITCHEN
10 minutes
CHILLING *2 hours in the refrigerator*
STORAGE *up to 24 hours in the refrigerator*
serves 4

whites of 4 eggs
pinch of salt
250 g / 8 oz bittersweet chocolate
1 orange
30 g / 1 oz sugar
6 tablespoons double cream
2 tablespoons Grand Marnier or other orange-flavoured liqueur

food mixer
4 mousse pots or ramekins

What makes a chocolate mousse memorable is less the time and trouble you take than the quality of the chocolate you use. The top brands vary quite surprisingly in flavour: some being creamy, others spicy with a nip of bitterness. Personally I like the smoky taste of chocolate that has a high cocoa content. This particular recipe is based on ganache — *a classic cake filling of chocolate melted in cream — which is lightened with whipped egg whites. You can vary the orange flavour of the mousse by substituting a different liqueur, such as crème de menthe for mint, or Kahlua for coffee.*

Bring about 2.5 cm / 1 in of water to the boil in a small saucepan for a water bath. Put the egg whites into the mixer with a pinch of salt to help them break up and rise. Whisk them stiffly — no need for any work by hand, the mixer does a good job here. Leave the whites whisking while you chop the chocolate.

Break it into chunks, then chop it in the food processor or using a large knife. Put the chocolate into a small heatproof bowl and set it over the water bath to melt.

With a vegetable peeler, pare a strip of zest from the orange and finely grate the rest.

When the egg whites are stiff, add the sugar and continue to whisk for about 30 seconds, until they turn glossy and form a light meringue with shallow peaks when the whisk is lifted. Set them aside.

Make the ganache: bring the cream to the boil in a small pan and pour it over the chocolate. Let it stand for 15 seconds over the water bath, then stir until the chocolate is melted and smooth. Take it from the water bath and stir in the liqueur and grated zest.

Add the chocolate mixture to the meringue and fold gently until thoroughly mixed. Don't worry if the chocolate is still warm, it will cook the meringue slightly and help to stiffen it. Pour the mousse into mousse pots or ramekins. If you don't have either, use a stemmed glass or some pretty demi-tasse coffee cups — chocolate mousse should be presented as a frivolity.

Cover the mousse and chill for at least 2 hours to set; it keeps well and the flavour will mellow. If it separates slightly on standing, don't worry, the liquid will have an agreeable tang of the liqueur.

When serving, cut the piece of orange zest into 4 thin strips. Knot them, set one on each mousse and serve them on individual plates.

RECAP

1 BRING WATER TO BOIL IN SMALL SAUCEPAN. ADD PINCH OF SALT TO EGG WHITES AND STIFFLY WHIP.

2 MEANWHILE, CHOP CHOCOLATE. PUT IN SMALL HEATPROOF BOWL AND SET OVER WATER BATH.

3 PARE ONE STRIP OF ZEST FROM ORANGE. GRATE REST.

4 ADD SUGAR TO EGG WHITES AND CONTINUE WHIPPING **30** SECONDS UNTIL GLOSSY. SET ASIDE.

5 MAKE GANACHE: BRING CREAM TO BOIL IN SMALL SAUCEPAN AND POUR OVER CHOCOLATE. LEAVE BOWL OVER WATER BATH **15** SECONDS, THEN STIR UNTIL SMOOTH TO MAKE GANACHE. STIR IN LIQUEUR AND

ORANGE ZEST. ADD GANACHE TO MERINGUE AND FOLD GENTLY UNTIL THOROUGHLY MIXED.

6 POUR INTO POTS, COVER AND CHILL AT LEAST 2 HOURS.

7 TO SERVE, CUT STRIP OF ZEST INTO 4 THIN STRIPS. KNOT STRIPS AND SET ONE ON EACH MOUSSE.

WHITE WINE GRANITA WITH BLACKBERRIES

TIME IN KITCHEN
12 minutes
FREEZING *at least 3 and
up to 12 hours*

serves 4

Alcohol and sugar inhibit the freezing of liquid, so I guess I should not be surprised that sweet white wine freezes to make a perfect crumbling granita with the texture of lightly frozen snow. Unlike most granita mixtures, the wine need not be whisked as it chills, but you do need to allow about 3 hours for the wine to freeze before serving the granita.

A rich muscat wine such as Beaumes de Venise makes excellent granita, as do its cousins Montbazillac and Frontignan. California is now producing rich white wines from late-picked grapes, and the botrytis vintages of Australia offer further possibilities. All tend to be expensive, but a half bottle is all you need. We add further flavour to the wine by infusing it with juniper and cinnamon, a pungent foil for the blackberries (blackcurrants or blueberries are good alternatives). Don't forget a crisp biscuit or two to complete the treat.

½ **bottle**
   (375 ml / 12 fl oz)
   sweet white wine
50 g / 1¼ oz sugar
15 g / ½ oz juniper
   berries
2 cinnamon sticks
375 g / ¾ lb
   blackberries

*4 large coupe or
   stemmed glasses*

Put wine, sugar and 125 ml / 4 fl oz of water in a pan and bring to the boil over a high heat. Books will tell you not to do this as the sugar may not dissolve properly, but here we have plenty of liquid. If you stir once or twice as it comes to a boil, it will do fine.

Meanwhile, wrap the juniper berries loosely in plastic film or a plastic bag and crush them by pounding with a rolling pin or the base of a heavy pan. Add them to the wine syrup together with the cinnamon, lower the heat and simmer for 5 minutes. Take off the heat and leave to infuse for 2 minutes, or longer if you have the time.

While the syrup is simmering, pick over the blackberries, discarding stems. Leave them, uncovered, to chill in the refrigerator. Wash the blackberries only if they are dirty and do so at the last minute, drying them on paper towels.

Strain the infused wine syrup into a shallow glass, pottery or stainless steel dish to form a 2 cm / ¾ in layer. Cover it with plastic film and chill it in the freezer. Beware of using metal containers other than stainless steel for wine and other acid mixtures as they easily pick up a metallic taste.

Leave the granita to freeze for at least 3 hours, until it is firm and snowy with crystals. The exact time will depend on the temperature of your freezer and you can safely leave the granita an extra 2-3 hours without spoiling the texture. If left for more than 12 hours, however, it tends to lose its soft texture. Chill the glasses in the freezer.

Just before serving, pile the blackberries in the chilled glasses. With a fork, scrape the granita into soft chunks and pile them on the fruit. Set the glasses on plates – on napkins or doilies so they do not slip – add a biscuit on the side and serve at once.

WHITE WINE GRANITA WITH ROSEMARY

Granita is good any time of the year and as the seasons change you can vary the herbs, spices and even the wine you use in it. In summer I like to use a sprig of rosemary, snipped from the herb garden, and a few ripe nectarines.

In the recipe above, replace the juniper berries and cinnamon sticks with 2 large sprigs of rosemary. Pound the rosemary in the same way and finish the granita as described. Replace the blackberries with 2 or 3 medium nectarines. Wash them and wipe dry. Cut them in half following the indentations. Twist the halves apart and discard the stones. Lay each half cut side down and cut into 3-4 slices. Cut the slices in half to make dice. Serve the granita in chilled glasses as described.

RECAP

1 BRING WINE, SUGAR AND 125 ML / 4 FL OZ WATER TO BOIL OVER HIGH HEAT, STIRRING ONCE OR TWICE.

2 MEANWHILE, WRAP JUNIPER BERRIES LOOSELY IN PLASTIC FILM AND CRUSH WITH ROLLING PIN. ADD TO WINE SYRUP WITH CINNAMON STICKS AND SIMMER 5 MINUTES. LEAVE TO INFUSE 2 MINUTES LONGER, MORE IF TIME.

3 PICK OVER BERRIES AND CHILL, UNCOVERED. RINSE ONLY IF NECESSARY, JUST BEFORE SERVING.

4 STRAIN INFUSED SYRUP INTO SHALLOW GLASS BAKING DISH, COVER WITH FILM AND CHILL IN FREEZER ABOUT 3 HOURS UNTIL FIRM AND LIGHTLY CRYSTALLIZED. YOU CAN LEAVE UP TO 12 HOURS IN FREEZER. CHILL GLASSES.

5 JUST BEFORE SERVING, PILE BERRIES IN CHILLED GLASSES. WITH A FORK, SCRAPE GRANITA INTO SOFT CHUNKS AND PILE ON FRUIT. SERVE AT ONCE, WITH BISCUITS ON SIDE.

TIPSY BREAD & BUTTER PUDDING

TIME IN KITCHEN
10 minutes
BAKING *50-60 minutes*
STORAGE *up to 2 days in the refrigerator*

serves 4-6

175 g / 6 oz dry crusty loaf
45 g / 1½ oz seedless raisins
125 ml / 4 fl oz rum or whisky
375 ml / 12 fl oz milk
unsalted butter for the dish
4 eggs
100 g / 3¼ oz sugar
½ teaspoon vanilla essence

1.5 litre / 2⅓ pt baking dish

Good bread and butter pudding depends on the bread — it must be at least a day old, dry and chewy. Plenty of crust is important because it adds colour as well as texture to the pudding. You can go for French baguette, Italian ciabatta or simply a good white or brown home-made loaf. The other distinguishing feature of bread and butter pudding is the mix of flavourings — raisins are a must and vanilla is a good idea. The raisins invite a touch of rum or whisky, which here we're mixing directly into the custard which soaks the bread. Servings are generous, but leftovers never come amiss and no accompaniment is needed, though you might welcome a scoop of ice-cream.

Preheat the oven to 190°C/375°F/gas5, allowing 5 minutes for this before you start.

To give a different texture to bread and butter pudding, I like to tear the bread into 2.5 cm / 1 in chunks, rather than slicing it with a knife. Put the chunks in a large bowl with the raisins and pour over the rum or whisky and about two-thirds of the milk. Use your hands to squeeze the chunks of bread until they have fully absorbed the liquid, then leave them to soak. Butter the baking dish — I find the simplest way is to trap a bit of butter in paper towel and rub it around the dish.

Whisk the eggs in a large bowl with the sugar and vanilla just until smooth. Whisk in the remaining milk. Pour this custard over the bread and stir gently.

Pour the mixture into the prepared baking dish and spread it to a fairly even layer — it should be about 4 cm / 1½ in deep so the pudding has a crispy top and soft centre when it is baked. Make sure there are not too many raisins on top as they tend to dry out during baking.

Bake the pudding in the preheated oven for 50-60 minutes, until the custard is set and the top of the pudding is crisp and brown. A skewer inserted into the centre of the pudding should come out clean and be hot to the touch.

Serve it very warm but not scalding hot, plain or with ice-cream.

APPLE BREAD & BUTTER PUDDING

A quieter, more domestic version of Tipsy Bread & Butter Pudding.

In the recipe above, add 2 tart apples and replace the rum or whisky with 125 ml / 4 fl oz more milk. While the bread is soaking, halve and core the apples without peeling them. Dice them and stir into the bread with the raisins.

RECAP

1 PREHEAT OVEN TO 190°C/375°F/GAS5, ALLOWING 5 MINUTES FOR THIS BEFORE YOU START.

2 TEAR BREAD INTO CHUNKS, PUT IN A LARGE BOWL WITH RAISINS AND POUR OVER RUM OR WHISKY AND ABOUT TWO-THIRDS OF MILK. BUTTER BAKING DISH.

3 WHISK EGGS WITH THE SUGAR AND VANILLA UNTIL SMOOTH AND WHISK IN REMAINING MILK. STIR THIS CUSTARD INTO BREAD.

4 TIP MIXTURE INTO PREPARED DISH, SPREADING IT TO AN EVEN 4 CM / 1½ IN LAYER.

5 BAKE 50-60 MINUTES UNTIL PUDDING IS SET WITH BROWN CRISPY TOP; A SKEWER INSERTED IN CENTRE SHOULD COME OUT CLEAN. SERVE WARM.

See page 123

BRETON BUTTER CAKE

TIME IN KITCHEN
14 minutes
BAKING *35-45 minutes*
STORAGE *up to 3 days in
an airtight container*
serves 6-8

250 g / ½ lb flour
250 g / ½ lb unsalted
    butter, plus more for
    the tin
250 g / ½ lb caster sugar
6 eggs

*22.5 cm / 9 in tart tin
with removable base*

*Just think of Breton Butter Cake as the very best buttery shortbread you've ever tasted.
You don't need a bowl to mix it as it is worked like French pastry on a flat surface to form
a soft dough, which bakes like a chewy biscuit.*

*It keeps well for two or three days in an airtight container. You can eat it alone,
or with berries or fruit compote. Remember, unsalted butter makes all the difference to this
recipe — do not use salted varieties.*

Preheat the oven to 175°C/350°F/gas4, allowing 5 minutes for this before you start.
The butter should be at room temperature so it is easier to mix. Brush the tart tin with
a little butter.

Dump the flour in a pile on the work surface — I don't bother sifting, given
the kneading that is to come. Holding your hand like a paddle, sweep a large well,
25 cm / 10 in or so across, in the centre of the flour to hold the other ingredients.

Add the sugar and butter to the centre of the well. Separate the eggs and drop all
but one of the yolks in with the butter and sugar. Using the egg shell, cut one egg yolk
reserving about half of it in the shell for glaze and adding the rest. (Use the whites for
Marmalade Soufflé, page 116.) Have a pastry scraper or metal spatula handy.

Mix the ingredients in the centre of the well by pinching them with the fingertips
of one hand, rather like the pecking of a bird. After 1-2 minutes they will be soft and
sticky. Gradually pull in the flour with the scraper. Keep mixing with your fingers and
the scraper until the dough starts holding together like rough pastry. Keep on mixing
— the dough will soften and, after 2-3 minutes, it will form a smooth sticky paste.

Lift the paste with the scraper and drop it in the tart tin. Wash your hands, leaving
them wet. Make a fist and press the dough flat in the tin. Drop the reserved egg yolk
on the dough and brush it all over as glaze. Mark it in a lattice with the underside of a
fork — this is the classic decoration for Breton Butter Cake.

Bake the cake for 35-45 minutes, until it is golden brown, firm in the centre and
just starting to pull away from the sides of the tin. Don't over-bake or it will be dry.

Leave it to cool in the tin. When tepid, set the tin on a bowl or mug and the sides
will slide off. With a metal spatula, slide the cake from the base on to a serving plate
to be cut at the table. It is equally delicious slightly warm or cool.

RECAP

1 PREHEAT OVEN TO 175°C/350°F/GAS4, ALLOWING 5 MINUTES FOR THIS. THE BUTTER SHOULD BE AT ROOM TEMPERATURE. BRUSH TIN WITH LITTLE BUTTER.

2 DUMP FLOUR ON WORK SURFACE AND SWEEP A WELL IN CENTRE WITH HAND. ADD BUTTER, SUGAR AND EGG YOLKS, RESERVING HALF OF ONE FOR GLAZE. MIX WITH FINGERTIPS OF ONE HAND 1-2 MINUTES UNTIL SMOOTH. DRAW IN FLOUR AND CONTINUE MIXING 2-3 MINUTES TO FORM A SMOOTH, STICKY PASTE.

3 DROP INTO PREPARED TIN, WET FIST AND FLATTEN DOUGH UNTIL SMOOTH. BRUSH WITH RESERVED YOLK AND MARK A LATTICE PATTERN WITH FORK.

4 BAKE 35-45 MINUTES UNTIL GOLDEN BROWN AND JUST STARTING TO PULL FROM SIDES OF TIN. LEAVE TO COOL IN TIN, THEN UNMOULD ON PLATE.

RASPBERRY & CHOCOLATE FOOL

TIME IN KITCHEN
14 minutes
CHILLING at least 1 hour
and up to 24 hours in
the refrigerator
serves 4

250 ml / 8 fl oz double
cream
30 g / 1 oz bittersweet
chocolate
250 g / ½ lb raspberries
2 tablespoons kirsch or
lemon juice
60 g / 2 oz sugar, or
more to taste
15 g / ½ oz flaked or
slivered almonds

food mixer
4 large stemmed glasses

'Fool' has nothing to do with foolish. Dictionaries link its origins to that other British favourite, trifle; but I'm convinced the name comes from the French fouler, to whisk, which is what it takes to make this dessert. Tart fruit is best for fool — poached rhubarb and gooseberry rival raspberry and strawberry in popularity. To add texture, I've layered the fool with almonds and grated chocolate.

Perfect party fare, served with Breton Butter Cake (page 121).

As a precaution against cream curdling, I like to chill the mixer whisk and bowl in the freezer for 5-10 minutes before I start the recipe. The cream and glasses for serving should be chilled in the refrigerator.

Grate the chocolate on to a piece of paper or a plate. One easy way is to scrape the side of the chocolate with a vegetable peeler, like peeling a potato. Otherwise grate the chocolate using the coarse grid of a grater.

Put the cream in the chilled bowl and start whisking at medium speed. While tending to the raspberries, keep an eye on the cream. Once it starts to stiffen, watch it closely until it is thick enough to hold a soft peak when the whisk is lifted.

Meanwhile, pick over the raspberries, rinsing them with cold water in a strainer only if they seem dusty as water soaks them and spoils the texture. Purée about two-thirds of the raspberries in the food processor if you have one. Then, to remove the seeds, work them through a strainer into a bowl, using a wooden spoon. The processor saves time but you can also work the raspberries directly through the strainer.

Stir in the kirsch (use lemon juice if you are cooking for children) and sugar and taste, adding more sugar if you like. Set the remaining raspberries aside.

Add the raspberry purée to the cream and fold the two together lightly but thoroughly to make the fool. As you fold, the cream will thicken a little more because of the acid in the purée.

To assemble the dessert: spoon the raspberry fool into the chilled glasses, letting it fall from a height so it does not catch on the sides; fill the glasses about one-third full. Sprinkle the fool with half of the chocolate, half of the almonds, and 2-3 raspberries per glass. Add more fool, then a second layer of the remaining chocolate and almonds with a few more raspberries, reserving 4 for decoration. Fill with the remaining fool and top each glass with a single raspberry.

Chill for at least 1 hour and up to a day if you wish. The flavour of the fool will improve as it stands, though some liquid may separate to the bottom.

STRAWBERRY & CHOCOLATE FOOL

The flavour of sun-ripened strawberries marries wonderfully with cream, so don't even think of making this recipe with out-of-season berries.

In the recipe above, substitute the same weight of strawberries for raspberries. Hull the strawberries and purée two-thirds of them as described. Slice the rest, reserving 4 of the best for topping. Finish the recipe as directed.

RECAP

1 CHILL MIXER WHISK AND BOWL IN FREEZER 5-10 MINUTES BEFORE YOU START. CHILL CREAM AND SERVING GLASSES IN REFRIGERATOR.

2 GRATE CHOCOLATE WITH VEGETABLE PEELER OR GRATER. WHISK CREAM IN MIXER UNTIL IT HOLDS SOFT PEAKS.

3 MEANWHILE, PICK OVER RASPBERRIES, RINSING ONLY IF DUSTY. PURÉE ABOUT TWO-THIRDS IN PROCESSOR AND WORK PURÉE THROUGH STRAINER INTO BOWL TO REMOVE SEEDS. STIR IN KIRSCH OR LEMON JUICE AND SUGAR TO TASTE. SET REMAINING RASPBERRIES ASIDE.

4 WHEN CREAM HOLDS SOFT PEAKS, ADD RASPBERRY PURÉE AND FOLD TOGETHER TO MAKE FOOL.

5 FILL GLASSES ABOUT ONE-THIRD FULL WITH FOOL. SPRINKLE WITH HALF CHOCOLATE AND ALMONDS AND 2 OR 3 RASPBERRIES PER GLASS. ADD MORE FOOL, THEN A LAYER OF REMAINING CHOCOLATE, ALMONDS AND RASPBERRIES, RESERVING 4 RASPBERRIES FOR DECORATION. FILL THE GLASSES WITH REMAINING FOOL AND TOP WITH RASPBERRIES.

6 CHILL AT LEAST 1 HOUR BEFORE SERVING.

STRAWBERRY BURNT CREAM

TIME IN KITCHEN
14 minutes

serves 4

This is not crème brûlée, *nor even a version of* crème brûlée, *but a dish of strawberries and cream with a brown sugar topping. The strawberries are blanketed with whipped cream, sprinkled thickly with dark brown sugar and grilled — yes, grilled! Under the fierce heat the sugar melts to become a crunchy lattice, the cream foams and browns lightly, and the strawberries heat just enough to be warm. Serve at once. Other fruits such as blueberries, sliced peaches and pears also do well in this delicious, original dessert.*

500 ml / 16 fl oz double cream
750 g / 1½ lb strawberries
250 g / ½ lb dark brown sugar

food mixer
shallow baking dish

Preheat the grill. Chill the food mixer whisk and bowl in the freezer, allowing 5-10 minutes for this before you start the recipe. The cream should also be chilled in the refrigerator.

Put the cream in the chilled bowl and start beating at medium speed. After 2-3 minutes the cream will start to thicken. Then watch it closely until it is firm enough to hold a stiff peak when the whisk is lifted. If over-whisked it will curdle and turn to butter, though there's little danger of this if the cream was well chilled in advance. A yellow tinge and slightly rough texture are danger signals — stop whisking at once.

While the cream is whisking, hull the strawberries, rinsing them in a colander under cold water only if they are sandy. Water tends to soak them, spoiling their texture. Arrange them in an even layer in the baking dish. They should all touch the bottom and if any are very large, halve them.

When the cream is stiff, spread it over the strawberries with a spatula, covering them completely. If you want to prepare an hour or two ahead, chill the dessert in the refrigerator at this point.

With your fingers, crumble the brown sugar over the cream in as even a layer as possible, if necessary spreading it with the spatula. Put it as close as possible to the grill, not more than 5 cm / 2 in from the heat, and grill for 3-4 minutes. At first the sugar will melt, then start to sink into the soft bubbling cream as it caramelizes. Once the cream is well browned, the dessert is ready.

Set it on a plate and rush it to the table in the manner of a soufflé.

RECAP

1 PREHEAT GRILL. CHILL MIXER WHISK AND BOWL IN FREEZER, ALLOWING 5-10 MINUTES FOR THIS BEFORE YOU START.

2 START WHISKING CREAM AT MEDIUM SPEED. MEANWHILE, HULL STRAWBERRIES, WASHING ONLY IF SANDY. SPREAD IN BAKING DISH, HALVING ANY THAT ARE LARGE. WHEN CREAM HOLDS STIFF PEAKS, SPREAD OVER STRAWBERRIES.

3 WITH YOUR FINGERS, CRUMBLE BROWN SUGAR OVER CREAM, SPREADING AS EVENLY AS POSSIBLE. GRILL VERY CLOSE TO HEAT FOR 3-4 MINUTES UNTIL SUGAR HAS MELTED AND CREAM STARTS TO BROWN. SERVE AT ONCE.

MACERATED PEACHES

TIME IN KITCHEN
4 minutes
MACERATING *1 hour, or*
up to 24 hours in the
refrigerator

1 bottle
   (750 ml / 27 fl oz)
   fruity red wine
100 g / 3½ oz sugar,
   or more to taste
1 lemon
½ teaspoon vanilla
   essence
4 large peaches
   (about 750 g / 1½ lb)
biscotti or amaretti for
   serving

These peaches macerated in red wine, lemon and sugar should be served with biscotti or amaretti biscuits for dipping in the juice. The recipe dates back to medieval times and was called chicolle, *meaning a purée or gruel thick enough to eat easily with a spoon. You can eat the peaches almost at once, but a lengthy maceration will improve them — 12-24 hours is ideal. Be sure to use a fruity red wine — Zinfandel does well, as do many reds from the Rhône valley. Try strawberries macerated like this too.*

Pour the wine into a medium serving bowl and stir in the sugar. Pare the zest from the lemon as thinly as possible, using a vegetable peeler. Be careful not to include the white pith as it can be bitter. Twist each strip of zest over the wine to release the lemon oil and drop it into the wine. Add the vanilla and stir for 20-30 seconds to encourage the sugar to dissolve in the wine.

The reason this recipe is so quick is that I don't bother to peel the peaches. I find that soaking them in wine softens all but the thickest of skins. First divide the peaches in half: following the indentation, cut around the fruit down to the stone. Twist with both hands to loosen the halves. Freestone peaches will separate easily, but if they are the clingstone type, you may need to use a knife. (You cannot judge type by looking at the fruit, so read the label carefully.) Scoop out and discard the stones.

Cut each half into 5-6 crescent-shaped slices, letting them fall into the wine syrup. Stir gently to mix fruit and syrup and set a plate on top so the fruit is completely immersed. Chill for at least 30 minutes and up to a day.

Just before serving, remove the plate and taste the syrup, adding more sugar if you like. Wipe the edge of the bowl with paper towel to clean it and serve the macerated peaches in the bowl. Pass biscotti or amaretti biscuits separately, leaving guests to dip them into their individual bowls.

RECAP

1 POUR WINE INTO MEDIUM SERVING BOWL AND STIR IN SUGAR. PARE ZEST FROM LEMON AND TWIST EACH STRIP BEFORE DROPPING IT INTO SYRUP. STIR IN VANILLA.

2 CUT PEACHES IN HALF, FOLLOWING INDENTATION, AND TWIST TO LOOSEN FROM STONES. DISCARD STONES. CUT EACH HALF INTO 5-6 SLICES, LETTING THEM FALL INTO SYRUP.

3 SET PLATE ON THE PEACHES SO THEY ARE IMMERSED IN SYRUP AND CHILL AT LEAST **30** MINUTES AND UP TO A DAY.

4 JUST BEFORE SERVING, REMOVE PLATE AND TASTE THE SYRUP, ADDING MORE SUGAR IF NEEDED. SERVE MACERATED PEACHES IN BOWL, WITH BISCOTTI OR AMARETTI PASSED SEPARATELY.

MENUS IN AN HOUR OR LESS

The recipes in this book each take not more than 15 minutes of your kitchen time, so in less than an hour you can put together a generous meal with two or three dishes and still leave time to wash up and set the table. Here are just a few suggested menus, some to prepare partly or completely ahead, and others to make at the last minute for more relaxed occasions. The order of work is the one I find suits me best. All the menus serve four people, and you'll see that some can easily be doubled.

DINNER WITH FRIENDS

It's possible to make this dinner in just an hour before serving, but I prefer a more relaxed approach, cooking the chicken ahead so the flavour has time to mellow. The sauce is spicy, asking for the classic Oriental accompaniment of boiled rice. The dessert of individual Marmalade Soufflés takes less than 10 minutes to bake, so prepare them before dinner and keep them in the refrigerator while you serve the first two courses.

Chicory Salad with Goats' Cheese Toasts (page 87)
Chicken in Chilli Coconut Sauce (page 26)
Marmalade Soufflé (page 116)

Up to 2 days ahead: cook chicken and refrigerate.
Half an hour before dinner: prepare chicory, dressing and cheese toasts.
20 minutes before: put rice to boil; warm chicken over low heat; make soufflés and chill.
10 minutes before: drain rice, spread in buttered dish, cover and keep warm; grill toasts.
5 minutes before: toss salad, pile on plates and add toasts; turn off heat and leave chicken to keep warm.
After serving chicken: bake soufflés.

LAST-MINUTE SUPPER I

Chaudrée, the Breton ancestor of fish chowder, is a wonderful one-pot meal laden with cod, mussels, potatoes and onions, all simmered in clam juice and cream. While it's cooking, there's time to make a simple dessert of sliced oranges, topped with a crunchy caramel, to complete a light but satisfying meal.

Breton Chaudrée (page 30)
Orange Salad with Caramel (page 110)

Half an hour before: make chowder and leave to simmer 6-8 minutes.
15 minutes before: prepare oranges and caramel and chill.
Before serving oranges: sprinkle with crisp caramel.

LAST-MINUTE SUPPER II

This is a great autumn menu when wild mushrooms and pears are in season, though it will be welcome most of the year. I would add a green salad to go with the pasta, and ice-cream or biscuits with the pears (they are served warm as they continue to simmer while you're enjoying the main course). This is a good menu for large numbers as you can easily double or triple the recipes.

Bow-ties with Wild Mushrooms & Nuts (page 50)
Peppered Pears in Red Wine (page 106)

Half an hour before: prepare and poach pears.
20 minutes before: make wild mushroom sauce and cook bow-ties.
10 minutes before: wash salad greens, make dressing and toss salad.
Just before supper: drain bow-ties and toss with sauce and nuts.
During supper: check pears for cooking, remove them and leave syrup to simmer.
Before serving pears: transfer pears to serving bowls, add ice-cream if you like and spoon over hot syrup.

MAKE-AHEAD MOROCCAN DINNER

Two Moroccan recipes, a chicken *tajine* and sweet pastries filled with dried fruits, nuts and chocolate, combine well as an exotic dinner. You might open the meal with *mezze*, little dishes of olives, toasted almonds, toasted chick peas, crudités, perhaps some hummus and pitta bread from the deli. Serve the *mezze* with drinks before the meal, or as a first course at the table. No accompaniments are needed as aubergine is cooked with the chicken.

Tajine of Chicken with Aubergine (page 27)
Moroccan Dried Fruit & Chocolate Galettes
  (page 112)

Day before: cook tajine and refrigerate; bake galettes
  and store in an airtight container.
Half an hour before: reheat tajine in oven at
  180°C/350°F/gas4.
Before serving tajine: turn off oven and, if you like,
  leave galettes in oven to warm.
Before serving galettes: sprinkle with icing sugar.

A MENU FOR SUMMER

Colourful and refreshing, this menu will revive both you
and your guests on a hot day. Not only is little actual
cooking involved, the menu needs no accompaniment
except ice cubes for the *gazpacho*! Planning ahead, half
the preparation is done the day before, with only dessert
to assemble before the meal, be it lunch or dinner.

Red Wine Gazpacho (page 12)
Monkfish with Pancetta & Spinach (page 33)
Raspberry & Chocolate Fool (page 122)

Day ahead: prepare and chill gazpacho and fool.
35 minutes before: wrap monkfish in pancetta, tie and
  roast in oven.
7 minutes before: prepare and cook spinach.
Just before serving: test monkfish; when done, add
  spinach to pan, set roast on top and cover with foil,
  return to oven, turn off heat and leave to keep
  warm; spoon gazpacho into chilled bowls, add ice
  cubes and cucumber twists.
Before serving roast: discard strings, slice fish and
  arrange with spinach on platter or plates.
Before serving fool: top with raspberries.

A MENU FOR WINTER

Much of the cooking for this menu is done shortly before
serving the meal. Only the mousse is prepared ahead.
French bread is an appropriate accompaniment for both
the first and main courses, or you may want to bake
some potatoes for hearty appetites. While you are serv-

ing the first two courses, the pudding continues to bake
in the oven so it comes to the table piping hot. Custard
or ice-cream will complete the picture.

Chicken Liver & Apple Mousse (page 16)
Pork Chop with a Confit of Onions (page 40)
Tipsy Bread & Butter Pudding (page 120)

Up to 3 days ahead: make mousse and refrigerate.
45 minutes before: if serving baked potatoes, put them
  to cook; make onion confit and leave to simmer;
  cook pork chops and set aside.
30 minutes before: prepare and bake bread and butter
  pudding.
Before serving mousse: set pots of mousse on plates
  and slice bread as accompaniment; add chops to
  confit, cover and keep warm on top of stove.
Before serving chops: test pudding and, if done, turn
  off oven and leave to keep warm.

AN ITALIAN BRUNCH

With their light and lively flavours, so many Italian
recipes are ideal for brunch. Here I suggest only three,
but you'll find many more in this book. The granita is
prepared ahead, with the other two recipes made in the
morning to serve together as one course. Just add some
good bread, and you're ready to sit down at table.

Frittata with Spinach & Goats' Cheese (page 98)
Quick Ratatouille (page 91)
White Wine Granita with Blackberries (page 118)

Evening before: mix and freeze granita.
45 minutes before: prepare frittata and leave to cook.
30 minutes before: make ratatouille and leave at room
  temperature; pick over blackberries, pile in glasses
  and chill.
Before serving frittata and salad: slice bread; transfer
  frittata to platter or plates.
Before serving granita: scrape granita into chunks
  and pile on blackberries.

INDEX